# The Push For African-Centered Education:

## An Educator's Guide

Cassandra J. St. Vil

ISBN-13: 978-1548015251

# THE PUSH FOR AFRICAN-CENTERED EDUCATION: AN EDUCATOR'S GUIDE

A guide to understanding Black identity development and incorporating cultural relevance in the high school setting.

CASSANDRA J. ST. VIL, MSW, MS. ED, PH. D.

# CONTENTS

# PREFACE

First, I will admit that this idea is all wrong. Wrongfully projected as a global issue anyway. Race is a social construct, but no other country (or continent, really) makes race out to be as restrictive as in the U.S. Yet, isn't that the major grievance in privilege in the first place? The hegemonic voice (that which is in power) trumps others. In the case of race, our interpretation of this categorical system is seen in the global context as if affects the rest of the world in the same way. Not true.

Here's our issue: in the U.S., we have leaned on race to identify and reinforce racial categories and further, stereotypes, to better our social understanding. Black identity has been entirely mishandled and created as ugly or lacking for centuries since. Accordingly, then, it is usually ignored. If studied, it becomes this imagined thing: a catchall box to put all things we refuse to learn more about.

*An object to be studied- a topic, rather than a people impacted by the categories they have been forced into.*

We create and live by false definitions of Black identity: skin color, behavior, ancestry, origin or place of birth. These are false, of course, because there are outliers and exceptions in each. For instance, all Black people aren't the same skin color.

My entire premise is to reposition how we view Black identity in America. By speaking from a positive standpoint, we can replace this negative ideology around Blackness that usually leads to racism, discrimination, marginalization and separation from what we have created as "other." By finally celebrating it, we can begin to see Black identity in contribution to American society, history and people. The problem with this is that past misunderstandings of Black identity has led to poor messaging of what Black identity is in social and academic spaces. In schools, we handle Blackness in a largely negative and removed way. To heal from that, I am proposing a high school curriculum which includes Black identity in positive light across the curriculum and school culture... but what does that even mean? What does it mean to reposition Black identity in a positive frame?

In enters all of the ways in which we have defined Blackness, again highlighting people from a particular area or shade of skin color, which inadvertently reinforces stereotypes and ignores outliers. Most popularly, we create a Black = African connection, geographically aiming to have Africa fill a need for positive identity development among U.S. Blacks and name a place, a land to it.

Here are the issues with Africa = Black: Not all Africans are Black. Really. Non-Black Africans have been on the continent for CENTURIES. If a white person, by our understandings of race, is born and raised in an African country, are they or are they not African?

Not all Africans identify as Black. I wrote this preface while I was in Mauritius, engaging with educators from all over the African continent. The repeated and resounding message when I was proposing my work about Black identity was that the U.S. discusses race as salient identities, particularly around the Black identity. Potentially, the U.K does something similar. But a million other identities are much more present than race, like language spoken, religion or ethnic group, or region of a particular country. On the island, itself are the descendants of indentured servants (largely from India) and descendants of slaves. Geographically, it sits in the Indian Ocean near, but not directly next to southeastern Africa. That said, many Mauritians may not see themselves in connection to Africa or an

African identity, and likely not to a Black race. To then create a Black super-group, a social construct that Africans need to step into in order to belong to a global body of people who may look like them ignores the outliers (i.e. Africans who aren't Black, and Africans who prioritize identities other than race in their lives).

Africa has over 50 countries, countless numbers of languages, and a million more cultural groups. Is it fair to refer to the continent of Africa as if it is just one thing (read: culture), just for the sake of having a palatable definition of what Black is in the U.S.? In other words, because the U.S. needs a starting point to define Blackness we choose a whole continent and make it out to be one singular thing: Africa. This way we can affix all of our (mis-) understandings of what this singular IT is, as if it is one thing.

To resolve all of these issues, I admit that this discussion is entirely centered around the U.S. construction of race and in particular, Black identity in the U.S. There has to be something to address how everyone who looks a certain way or comes from a particular country or continent or acts a certain way get permanently locked into stereotypical misunderstandings of Blackness. This something (ex. my position and the platform this book confronts) acknowledges that Black identity exists in the U.S. It asserts that Black identity has been misrepresented in the U.S., where Black identity has been stigmatized, excluded or distorted. It proposes curriculum to correct these misunderstandings. It recognizes a multitude of problematic definitions of Black identity. It introduces Black identity as a social-political group to step into. It acknowledges that some choose to step into this social-political group around Black identity while others may not. It realizes that some people are placed into this racial group based on social perceptions in the U.S. whether they choose to identify as Black or not. It deeply celebrates that Blackness therefore includes a wide variety and diversity in Blackness. It stresses that everyone, regardless of their identity as Black or not, can benefit from repairing their understandings of Black identity based on the misrepresentations the U.S. has maintained for so long. It offers a solution through a school option for students at a pivotal period of development and age bracket. It does not assert to be the end-all-be-all solution to racism toward Black identity.

Racism doesn't only exist in the U.S., that is for sure. But we in the U.S. handle race and racism in ways that don't always apply in other contexts. Race isn't always as raw, awkward, uncomfortable, suffocating and frightening in other places, countries and communities as the knot we have to disentangle and the elephant we have chosen to ignore in the U.S. Thus, I must say, aiming to reposition Black identity in the world may not be right, but it's right on time in the U.S.

# 1 GIVE A PERSONAL ACCOUNT

## Introduction

### An Opening

*I was entirely unaware of my Black identity.*

I grew up on the bordering edge of Jackson Heights, Queens, in what would actually be known as the most ethnically diverse town in the nation. "White" wasn't in my conversation, nor was it yet the center of all my discussions about power and identity. We were all racially, ethnically and religiously different. I was in *the* Haitian family on the block I grew up on, sandwiched between an elderly couple from Colombia on our left and a complex with Mexican-Puerto Rican families on the right. We shared a two-story townhome with a Dominican family on the first floor. We had a Jewish landlord, and Egyptian neighbors down the street. Not sure where Mariam was from exactly, but I think I remember her mother wearing hijab and speaking Arabic. Our street had a long-term stability unusual for the rental scene of New York City. My family lived on 85th Street more than ten years, a lifetime according to the city's standards. The only reason we finally moved from the apartment was because a major house fire had demolished nearly all of our belongings in 1999. *Otherwise, the kids on our street grew up together.* We played "Manhunt," climbed rooves, ran throughout the alleyway across the street from our rowhomes and baseball in the street whenever the car traffic was clear. We opened fire hydrants each summer, and jammed to HOT 97 on the radio.

*Confronting* race was not a part of my conversation yet either. If there were any comparisons made, it's that Black girls like me were slightly less pretty than all the Spanish girls in the neighborhood, largely to do with the wooliness of my hair. If your hair flowed like those Colombian, Puerto Rican and Mexican girls, you were doing alright. I wasn't too dark skinned, but my hair was indeed short, never without a perm since the age of nine. These were the things I came to understand as my status quo without anyone ever explicitly telling me outright. It was in the way I was treated and socially informed about my status, what was considered pretty and how I could best fit in. I sure do remember Mrs. Castro always yelling at me, in particular, for being unruly. I didn't do anything differently from my friends, but I was always the one called out for not having any manners by my grouchy next-door neighbor. She had never liked me, and I didn't want to spend too much time then trying decipher the reason why.

I remember accepting my tier pretty young. In terms of beauty, Latinas were highest. In terms of intelligence, Asians were highest. In terms of fitting in, Middle Easterners were most distinct (a.k.a. different) and kept to their own communities. As a tall, lanky Black girl from Queens, I was kind of cute, but simply not as a pretty as my Latina friends.... but I could learn the fun parts of Latina culture otherwise. I could roll my r's and learn how to salsa in a backyard with my Puerto Rican bestie, Cesar. I practiced my Spanish words like my Colombian friends taught me. I could cumbia like my Mexican friends, and plaster my bangs against my forehead with hair gel with the best of them "Puerto Rocks." In a protective community, where we all knew each other's families, economic class didn't matter as much.

I remember when I was twelve, I went on a service trip and stayed with a Black host family with two pre-teen daughters in St. Louis, Missouri. They gave me my first real perm and even though they used a box kit just like my mom did, my hair swayed and flowed like I had never experienced before then. Even out in Missouri, the message would become clear and consistent: wooly hair was unmanageable and had to be tamed by harsh chemicals that would make your hair sway in the wind like the Spanish girls on my block. I would rock my perms and hair straight until

I was a college student, having survived more than ten years of chemical relaxing. Sophomore year in college, however, I began to let the rough parts "out the kitchen," showing my grittier edges as new hair growth would surface desperately calling out for a relaxer I no longer used.[1][2]

We never really spoke about Blackness at home either, and if we did, it surely was something different than being Haitian. To be Black would mean violent, deceiving, thieving, uneducated and unruly. These messages were also never said out loud, but would become a part of my early understanding of what Blackness was. My mother would talk about the Black crime she saw on the news each night as "those kids" and all the challenges facing the "African-American community." At home, we were clearly Haitian, and not African American. But as the child of a single-immigrant mother, fitting in was top priority, thus English was spoken and burgers and fries were made.

It would have been too difficult for my mother's two children to balance both an English and Haitian identity, speaking both the English language and Haitian Creole or French. One of these identities had to be sacrificed, and since the ways of my mother's home country did not apply in our new context, becoming American meant shedding her

---

[1] A term I learned from my Puerto Rican friends raised in New York City.

[2] As an aside and point of pride, I haven't relaxed my hair since 2003 or 2004.

former ways. Since I was born in the U.S. I didn't really have former Haitian ways to get rid of. As a result, I never learned to speak Haitian Creole, unable to speak to anyone outside of my immediate family. I didn't learn Haitian customs or culture, save from an occasional dinner around the holidays and overhearing my mother's fluent conversations with her siblings. If Haitian-ness was *sauce pois avec zuri* and Black American-ness was black-eyed peas and rice, my brother and I learned how to eat spaghetti. I internalized this unspoken tier system as: "American" is higher than "Haitian" or "immigrant," but all of these labels are greater than "Black."

## The Quiet Messages

I've loved reading ever since my first copy (of what would become hundreds) of the Baby-Sitters Club novels by my then favorite author, Ann M. Martin. I read so much, academic performance and school testing came with easy success. To think, that white author led this little black girl right into the smart classes…entirely unaware of the tracking of students taking place at the same school. My class section would always have an art elective. We weren't the fine art painting kids in 6-1 or 6-2 or the band in 6-4, but surely classes 6-3, 7-3 and 8-3 were to be the best singers and the only classes to receive daily vocal trainings all three years of junior high school. It was an advantage to have already gained "smart skills" by this point in stratification. I was one of the few Black kids in my honors classes, although my middle school was also very diverse. I wasn't too aware of school tracking then, but all the bad kids and Black kids (generally, seen as synonymous then) were lumped into all of the later sections from 6-16 on through 6-23. I never even saw *those kids.* I didn't talk to him much then, but I also remembered my older brother in 8-23, the last class section among them. Their courses were held in the basement, teased for being in "C.S." classes, known to kids as "completely stupid." I still don't know what academics of the late nineties actually named C.S. to mean, but that message never got to us students. What was clear was that all the troublesome kids, largely the hot and spicy girls and rowdy boys were in *those classes*, and most of their "learning" was disciplinary.

I remember an old choir teacher I would have in middle school. All three years, she and I would have these horrific battles in class. Had she not learned that she would never win in a power struggle with a pre-pubescent 'tween?! It was a stage show performance in class almost every day. I had 70s and 80s after too many low grades in my music class, and a drop in overall GPA as a result. But I was in top honors, nonetheless. These weren't terrible grades, but I certainly wasn't eligible for top-tier and specialized schools in the city then.

I was tracked into high school in 1997. I would elect one of the premier schools for students who wanted to be teachers. My reading and writing had remained strong, spelling top-notch, which of course meant I wanted to be a high school English teacher. That was my first serious career goal right after wanting to be a ballerina. I hadn't started yet, but I just knew high school students to be cool, radical, smooth, sharp and exactly the kind of people I wanted to work with as a teacher.

## To Be Broken

*I fell apart at the age of fourteen.*

I had an anger in me so hot I thought it would burn through my chest for the world to see. I felt misunderstood. Damned all at the same time. I had barely stepped out of the gates of independence and was already knocked down by hatred, cynicism and racism.

I crashed into Washington Irving High School in September 1997. This historic school was centered in lower Manhattan, steps away from Union Square on the east side. In hindsight, I always wonder how many students have the major task and responsibility of commuting to and from a major business district for their schooling?! For a million reasons, this would be a crash course I did not yet need outside of my protective Queens bubble at the age of fourteen, whether the train station stop was so named 14th street or not. Of my one year at Washington Irving before transferring to a smaller high school in Queens in my 10th grade year, I wrote:

> *Freshman year in high school would be the first time I would be confronted with my racial grouping. My peers and I developed ideas of what to expect of each other, finding easy ways to sort into smaller groups and cliques based on commonalities. Race quickly became the defining feature in a school of more than 1,000 students, nine stories, metal detectors and window bars. Friendships were divided along racial categories- Blacks, Hispanics, Asians, Other; each had their own expectations and stigmas established by student racial group members themselves. Being a member of the Black group, however, came loaded with negative stereotypes of being disruptive in the classroom, disrespectful to teachers and administrators, and academically disengaged to maintain bravado and identification with the Black peer group. My largely Black peers challenged me to join them, and later shunned me when I didn't reinforce low expectations and negative behavior they associated with "being Black." The results of being an outlier at the critical period in identity development of adolescence were paramount. My grades plummeted where they were once lauded with academic honors. Prior to the end of freshman year, I disengaged entirely from all things, disconnecting from peers, teachers, family, and home life.*[3]

[3] This is an excerpt from my graduate admission essay to the Harvard Graduate School of Education. I was accepted, but this isn't a memoir, and I won't detail much how I spiraled from crisis to future academic and educator. Nonetheless, I hope some of the traces of my story help to inspire (your) work with urban youths. The premise behind this entire book being, "we can make it!"

I mostly remember the emotions of rage and loneliness best. I was so pissed off that people (my peers) couldn't see me for me. It was like failing the Black test to see if I was "Black enough" on a daily basis. Coming from Jackson Heights, I probably couldn't have been any more a fan of multiculturalism, but I certainly couldn't yet form a position on it at such a tender age. I think, in an unsure and unclear way, I believed in some sense of racelessness then. Yes, we are all different and come from varying identities (in my home community, anyway) but that didn't dictate your behavior or culture. In other, inexplicit thoughts, I don't have to be bad like Blacks. "I don't have to be anything at all, just me as an individual" was the best my freshman mind could formulate. I could not yet scrutinize the notion, "does Black actually have to mean bad?"

What we (my Black peers and I) didn't yet understand at the ages of fourteen and fifteen is that we were all grasping for connection. In a school setting so big, so different from our hometowns and smacked in lower Manhattan, we simply needed a synthesizing point. Race was the easiest among them, thus the Black kids had to act the same. This largely meant the negative stereotypes I hinted at earlier.

To be "Black enough" meant long finger nails and hair weaves or boxed braids with extensions, and a hot temper, particularly toward authority. Nothing in your accent could "sound white" which largely came with fast speech, animated movements of the neck, wild hand gestures and sucking your teeth when appropriate…which was often, because you were to always be upset or annoyed.

Needless to say, my grades fell to the ground, then many levels beneath it. I wore brown clothing from the start of the school year until the last school day that year. It was as close as I could get to gothic fashion style in a central Manhattan high school as a young Black girl. At first, it was my stylistic expression for color and style. I found the color brown to be so chic. It then easily represented my depression. This murky shade found in my soft faux leather jacket and Trapper Keeper binder, and all the brown sweaters or cheap boots or shoes I could find in a discount store captured my every lonely moment.

My mother, a single working mother from Haiti, had nothing to do with this. Her accented English was used to feed, clothe and care for her children as a home care attendant, shuffling elderly and immobilized persons throughout life's chores. She was ill aware of this emotional turmoil her youngest was experiencing in high school, nor was I going to tell her. I remember stealing her credit cards and shopping through her catalogs for clothes beyond my age. I ran away from home to stay with a good friend's Puerto Rican family in Spanish Harlem for a while. I would curse at my mom, yelling in the streets like it was acceptable to treat another human that way.

Even after I transferred high schools, I was scarred by the expectations of my peer group and suddenly very aware of my race, how people treated or mistreated me because of my race and how angry I was to notice the difference. I remember poor Ms. M, who would become my arch nemesis come tenth grade. Every word I said to her had a cuss in it, but who was she to continue to call out my name in that small French class?! My ego couldn't have grown bigger to mask my broken esteem. At my new school, I adopted all the stereotypes I had fought against at Washington Irving and giving teachers a tough time came with the territory.

I bounced along the remainder of high school, dramatically improving my grades and behavior the deeper I became involved with youth programming at the YMCA. I can say that their inclusive programs and clubs for city teens saved my life, and allowed me to meet all sorts of teenagers, throughout New York City, figuring out their identities as well. Without it, I would not have traveled to Eastern Europe in a cultural exchange service trip or win a college scholarship as a turnaround youth, recognized as New York City's YMCA Youth of the Year in 2001.

## Turning It Around

*I was the story.*

The turnaround case that youth workers dreamed of when designing programs and approaches to reach urban teens of color. Even still, I remember another Cohen I would meet in my life. This one, not my Jackson Heights landlord, but my high school guidance counselor, in this teeny, no window, two-story high school right next to a highway in Queens. After bringing my grades up more than twenty points (even to the occasional honor roll listing), Ms. Cohen, my guidance counselor senior year would tell me that Buffalo State College, my dream school for its social work program, wouldn't accept me. I never considered her comment to be anything other than race-related. By age 17, I was aware that some things didn't have to be said out loud. I was this mouthy Black girl in her eyes, and despite two years of steady academic growth, my grades and overall performance were not at par with the standards of any state school. She didn't replace the option with any other school choices either; she didn't suggest community college or really anything other than dutifully submitting New York City's citywide college applications not because I was a strong candidate, but because all exiting students needed to apply somewhere.

I went to Buffalo State in the fall of 1997, largely to spite Ms. Cohen. I applied for financial aid and completed most paperwork independent of my mother who had no clue what all these documents and numbers would mean. She would readily receive and pay any bill that came with it, but college was my own journey. My mother would send me care packages in the first year, receive my annual holidays visits with great cooking and shine proudly once I graduated…with academic honors four years later.

*I am Black in experience, and Africanist by profession.*

This isn't meant to be a memoir, otherwise I would outline the journey through my years at Buffalo State, and how a minor degree in African and African-American Studies there became my first exposure to anything positive about my racial group. I would tell the tales between my first master's program, my entry into a Ph.D. program in African Studies at the age of 23, or my entry into the classroom as a high school special education teacher after it. The shorter answer is I have elected to infuse Black identity uplift in my work with urban teens and have been since I learned how much my racial group had impacted my own adolescent and young adult development.

Whether the conversations were explicitly had or not, there was something unique in being a child of immigrants, yet alienated from extended family for not knowing the local language, behaviors, or food cast along with this. There was something wildly jarring about being lumped into the Black social group at school, without any understanding at all about what the group's membership meant, other than a checkbox on an application telling me where to tick or frightening associations of being bad, consistently angry and violent.

*Where do the Black kids go?*

We throw Black teenagers into a gaping hole, forgetting to explain to them what Blackness means. We assume they will get it at home, in their neighborhoods or other forms of connection with their cultural inheritance. We assume that a Black kid should be able to figure out what it means to be Black on their own. My standing question is, “is that so?” Are they able to figure it all out on their own? How? More so, where?

# 2 DISCUSS EXISTING APPROACHES

## The Premise

The purpose of my writing this is essentially two-fold:

My first attempt is to explain what everyone, globally, seems to have accepted as norm in the general distortion of Black identity and the histories and cultures of Black peoples.

The second aim being an offering of a worthy resort, at least in the United States' context, of how we can respond to this ongoing misrepresentation in our school systems by proposing a new academic model centering Black uplift.

Black is (NOT!) bottom.

I write this as member of the Black community. I have my own experience receiving distorted representations of my own Black identity, spoon-fed and delivered in my formative education, in my various communities and in my travels. But I also write this as a professional Africanist[4] having sought out correction and clarification of what Black identity really is; I have spent my adult career thus far picking at an ice block in trying to understand self-in-context. The problem being: we have so marginalized accurate reflections of Black histories across the globe, it becomes a looming task to uncover true perspectives.

In this work and truth-seeking, I have continuously landed upon the same theme impacting the way in which we interact with Black identity worldwide. This theme and widely accepted belief is that *black is bottom.* Although it is rarely said explicitly, we have globally accepted, across continents and over centuries, associations of Black African descendants and continentals as everything vile, ugly, sinister, inferior, less than and dangerous. What do I mean, exactly? Need proof?

---

[4] As an Africanist, I study the histories and cultures of Black African continentals and Diasporans as a chosen profession. I do this in a variety of ways, thus it cannot be wholly captured in another discipline such as sociology or anthropology. It is a field unto its own.

If you would, please tell me…

where, in the world, is it of particular *advantage* to be Black?

Now continuing along these lines,

where is it of particular *disadvantage* to be Black?

That the latter question generates a list far lengthier than the former is testament to the widespread acceptance of this "black is bottom" theory. In most places, disadvantage (in the form of economic, social or political disparity with other cultural groups) is expected for the respective Black community within it. Globally, it is expected and accepted that Blacks are at a disadvantage when compared to any other cultural group.

Why is it okay that Blacks are at the bottom social tier everywhere in the world? In a better scenario, the question would ideally be "why is there any bottom tier at all?" but the former question challenges us to consider not only our social stratification systems, but worldwide acceptance of a particular group having a negative and further, disenfranchised existence *no matter where they reside in the world.* Why have we made it okay (in other words, normative) to create Black identity as "the other?"

If the Black community weren't consistently "othered" then the question "where is it advantageous to be Black?" wouldn't garner such a short list in response (no, really, there are over 200 countries in the world. Is there anywhere that values or celebrates Blackness?).

This is a significant consideration because we most often see the opposite of cultural celebration, throughout history to the present: Black Britons live in violence-ridden areas of London. Black American students are on the lower ends of the achievement gap each year across subjects. Skin whitening and lightening is a common practice found in most body creams and lotions in Nigeria. The list goes on to show how the world does not value Blackness.

If I were to then replace Black with any other cultural group (i.e. women, Christian, white, Asian) and ask these same two questions, responses would grossly differ. In some places, you may be at an advantage for being a woman, or at a disadvantage for being Christian; responses largely varying across cultural groups and societies. However, across them, it remains true that Blackness is ill-regarded when compared to any other cultural group. The goal here isn't to create a new bottom base, but recognize there is an inherent prejudice against Black identity that has to, finally, be confronted.

In response, as an educator, I propose something different, used in order to substantiate the existence of incredible beings in Blackness, and aim to heal the massive baggage of internal trauma hauled upon the Black identity. I offer my positions in this text as my own, influenced by experiences in my own life and those I have encountered. In addition to my own example, I offer a school model to counteract damage we have already done by sustaining the BiB (black is bottom) epidemic this long, and hope to convey the fundamental purpose behind African-Centered Education.

I focus my work in the United States because it is where I was born, raised and am most familiar with. It is where I aim to continue in African-centered education in the high school setting, with foreseeable partnerships throughout the Black African Diaspora. My geographic focus, by no means, makes this solely a "U.S. issue," as we know that we can afford to shift attitudes towards Black identity across the globe.

## What is Black?[5]

First, I will define the key terms I will use in my writing, the most crucial term among them being Black. I've circled around this idea often when choosing which language pushes conversations

---

[5] Please note, that when we are discussing the sociopolitical group, "Black," I have elected to capitalize it respecting its appropriate title of a group. Race, a social conception and idea wouldn't merit capitalization, thus I would leave white people in lower case, unless titling it as the White race. Since it would be obnoxious to distinguish between black people belonging to the Black sociopolitical group, I have capitalized Black, anywhere it is used in this writing moving forward.

around Black identity further along. One of my favorite authors on the subjects of race, racism and identity development writes,

> "I refer to people of acknowledged African descent as Black. I know that African American is also a commonly used term, and I often refer to myself and other Black people born and raised in America that way. Perhaps because I am a child of the 1960s 'Black and beautiful' era, I still prefer Black. The term is more inclusive than African American, because there are Black people in the United States who are not African Americans-Afro-Caribbeans, for example- yet are targeted by racism and are identified as Black (Tatum, 1997)."

This quote raises quite a few questions as we converge ideas about what Black identity is. Is the best term, "Black" or should it be something different? However, issues are generated with each new direction we try. Let's say we use a historical term like Negro or colored person. Immediate issues arise: Negro has almost exclusively been used in the United States and parts of Latin Americare. Am I a "Negro" if I am born in Haiti or Jamaica and living in the United States? I may still *look* Black in appearance, but using a geographically-locked title like "Negro" excludes inner-group diversity. We can suggest the term "colored," because it has been used outside of the United States as well. The issue here is finding a common definition: The term "Colored" means something entirely different dependent upon whether you are speaking to an American description or say, a South African point of view of what Colored is.

How about other terms we use to reference Black peoples? Do we accept the prefixes of "Afro" or "Afri" associating our inheritance there in connection to the African continent? Our challenge there being, of course is, Africans are not exclusively Black. Through exploration, expansion, colonialism, imperialism, regeneration and outright land theft, non-Black peoples have been in Africa for centuries. Are they any less African after generations have enjoyed their birthright on African soil?

The other question that the Tatum quote alludes to is that Black equals American. Is that the case? Is it a term exclusive to the United States, despite the fact that Black peoples refer to themselves by said title in countless other places?

I can't say I am proposing a new definition of what Black is. I think that task has been picked at throughout the globe, and over centuries. It'd be audacious of me to think I could have that answer to so easily define and share with others. However, as an aware observer, I can share approaches that have emerged in a variety of attempts to understand what Black identity is. I can share a few ideologies that I have witnessed people employ, and somewhat similar to my comments earlier, attempt to confront the issues in shaping Black identity in particular ways. More than all this thinking about the many ways in which we define what Black is, I want to demonstrate why I concluded that Black is the best term for the idea I am proposing.

Please note: the next section can be pretty frustrating. It's written to have us each examine what we have come to understand as Black. It may be a helpful task to **define what you consider Black to be before continuing reading.** I ask you:

What is Black?

1. *Black by Appearance*

I can't say this is the most popular version of classification, but we have countless stories of how we have decided people were Black based on their skin color. I walk into any classroom and people associate my own cinnamon skin tone with being Black. We even try to "science it" by saying if you have any melanin in your skin you must be Black. Here's the flaw in that: Are all Blacks the same skin color or complexion? Is there a certain level of melanin that must be in the skin to be considered Black? Do I actually have to be darker than a brown paper bag?![6]

When we define Blackness by skin color or our false measure of melanin we fall short of the wide

[6] Travesty 1,009,234 towards Blackness: Black Americans were historically "tested" to see if they were light enough to participate in prestigious Black groups. I learned of this when reading more about a particular Black sorority in the U.S. but still haven't researched the extent to which is was practiced. Nonetheless, it has been rumored that those darker than a brown paper bag were too dark in complexion for membership and weren't allowed to join.

variety in Black complexion. This creates all sorts of internal conflicts and questions about being "Black enough." Stereotypes have been that light-skinned Blacks think they are socially above darker-skinned Blacks…or aren't dark enough to even be considered Black. Both of these are untrue, but permeate as a result of our linking Blackness to the color of your skin.

We then create titles for our lighter-skinned Black companions like "high yellow" and "light bright." Some identify positively with these nicknames, others are traumatized by them after being constantly questioned and qualified as to whether or not they are actually Black. Sorting this way, by skin color, also necessitates extremes. If there is an extremely light Black label or title, then there will be an equal label for extremely dark-skinned. These distinctions would be welcome if they weren't also shaded with negative terminology and references. For instance, who would really want to be likened to the color of tar as a compliment?

*2. Black by Origin*

So maybe then it is easier to define Blackness by origin, declaring that anyone *from* Africa is, indeed, Black. Here's where that sorting falls short: There's a long, floating theory that all human beings originate from land that is in current Africa. Does that then mean we are all African? Does that mean we are all Black?

*3. Black by Nationality*

On to nationality. If you are born in a Black country, then you are Black.

What is a Black country? Do you mean a country where the majority of its peoples are Black? I was born in the U.S. and Blacks are not the majority in demographic size, thus it can't be considered a Black country…does that mean I am not Black? What if your country has multiple cultural influences? In Trinidad, in the southern Caribbean, there are just as many Blacks as there are East Indian, and a large community of peoples mixed between these groups. Are they Black, Indian or both? If I am born Black, will I always be Black? How about Black peoples in Curacao or Venezuela who look just like Cape Verdeans (West Africans), but would be called "mixed" in the U.S. or considered "Coloured" in South Africa?

*4. Black by Ethnicity*

I am Haitian. Does that mean I am Black? What if I were Brazilian? Millions of enslaved Africans were brought to South and Central Americas in the slave trade. Are they Black? Are their ancestors Black? Is it my behavior that determines this? My knowledge of a particular country's customs? Are there Black customs or countries that can appropriately determine if I am demonstrating Black ethnicity?

*5. Black by Culture*

If you speak/dress/talk/act/eat... a certain way then you are Black.

We do this all the time! I also call this "Black by behavior." If I perform in a certain way, then I am somehow further along the spectrum of Blackness. This has scales both within the Black community, testing whether "I'm really down" and outside of the Black community assessing whether or not my behavior aligns with understandings of Blackness (usually associated with stereotypes).

Surprising to some, however, there isn't necessarily a Black culture. Black peoples exist all over the world with a million plus permutations of our socio-political group. Someone who is Black in Georgia (the U.S. state) is likely not to have the same culture as someone else who is Black in Germany. We assume it, sometimes in jest even, limiting the reality that the Black sociopolitical group has subgroups. These subgroups can include geographic location or nationality or ethnic makeup (i.e. Black Caribbeans). For instance, Haitians are generally perceived as Black, and often identify as Black. Yet, among the large number of Haitians living in the U.S., many do not identify as African American. They may face similar discrimination on the basis of their shared Black identity, but maintain a culture distinct from Black Americans, who are seen to have their own culture.

Culture (shared norms, customs, language, food, etc.) are assigned to Black cultural groups like Black Americans, Black Britons, Black Ghanaians, etc. But all Blacks don't have a shared language, common food or customs, distinctive physical features, abilities or inabilities. In application, can we actually endorse stereotypes that all Black people like chicken, are afraid or don't know how to swim, or know how to run fast? Is it true that all Black people have wooly hair, dark skin or are athletic? Can we stretch our questioning here to raise doubts to the stereotypes that Blacks then are inherently more violent, less intelligent or sexualized on the basis of their race (socially conceived) or membership within the Black sociopolitical group (self-identified plus general perception)? No, we cannot generalize any of these stereotypes to apply to all Black people as if there were one universal, Black culture.

I don't remember the great movie, Coming to America, by heart. I can't make fried chicken or mac and cheese for the life of me. Does that mean I am not Black? It's silly to say that someone is Black by culture, because there isn't one distinct Black culture. If there was, then Blacks in West Philadelphia would have the same culture as those on the south side of Chicago, and those would be similar to North Carolina or all Blacks on the East Coast. If we are really then connected as Black peoples, then Black Americans would further be similar to Blacks in Europe. Since that isn't the case, then no, there isn't a singular Black culture any of us can belong to.

6. *Black in Social Perception*

You see me as Black, therefore I am Black.

This is often defined by complexion (see Point 1 above) or assumed behaviors of Blacks, associated with a Black culture that doesn't exist (see Point 5 right before this).

7. *Self-Identifying as Black*

I see myself as Black, therefore I am Black.

Huge hole here: If I say I'm Black and you don't agree that I am, who is actually correct?

8. *Ancestry as Black*

In our history, we had a disgusting rule in the U.S. where chased the Blackness in people in ways to villainize them. We came up with the "one-drop rule" system to classify one another, stating that if any of your great grandparents were Black, you were too, regardless of appearance, self-identification or social perception. This, of course, demoralized people, who would disconnect from Blackness, so we have a number of people refusing to self-identify as Black. We can now marry across racial lines so people now look differently over generations. We can't merely define it along ancestral lines, without including appearance, social and self-perceptions as a result.

*9. Defaulting as Black*

I don't fit it any other racial group, therefore I am Black.

How helpful is this force-fitting to ideas of positive identity development and Black uplift?

*10. Black Parentage*

My parent(s) are Black, therefore I am Black.

Maybe.

## The Black Socio-Political Group

I poke holes in all of these examples not to demoralize or further disconnect anyone who see themselves as Black. I merely want to question how we arrived at this answer. In all of them, there are gaping holes which exclude some Black members on the basis of one aspect or another, like you weren't born in the right place or time, or aren't light or dark enough. Since all those notions are silly, I bring to light that the actual hanging construct of Blackness in itself is indeed, created. We came up with an idea, put a bunch of people in that ideological group and treated them in a particular way as if they were all the same…when they (Black peoples) are not.

Since the world has undergone centuries of this misunderstanding of Blackness, it has created a commonality among this imagined Black group.

Globally, Blackness is marginalized, stigmatized and abused. Accordingly, it should then galvanize as its own social-political group on the basis that is already treated as one. If people currently understand Blacks to be one way, and treat them a certain way, then the group should form to handle or respond to that reality. In other words, Blacks have to come together because they have been forced together for so long and equally terrorized as a group for ages. Who is Black in Madrid? Who is Black in Dar es Salaam? Who is Black in Cairo? Who is Black in Calcutta? Who is Black in Nairobi?

Regardless of how the conclusion is drawn, pigmentation, family line or otherwise, social perception has often led way into categorically placing Blacks in this super-Black box. This Black group is then mistreated on the basis of a construct that has been created and can be defined in at least ten different ways as described earlier. Diversity shows us that a Black person in Atlanta is culturally different from a Black person in Freetown; however, what unites them is the common plight for equality for Blacks in both cities.

I am proposing Blackness as a social identity. A socio-political group that doesn't require a membership card or dues. Our dues of belonging are often paid through the discrimination and marginalization experienced in our respective communities as member of a Black group. As a social-political group, it includes anyone of Black inheritance across the globe. It can encompass race, origin, ethnicity or complexion, but leaves room for a few confounding realities that not all Black people are dark-skinned, born on the African continent or seemingly, appear to be Black. In reality, all Black people aren't any one particular thing (way of being) other than seeing themselves as and/or being seen as Black. That's where the "social" end in sociopolitical grouping comes in. Blackness has to invite a level of identification where an individual identifies themselves to be Black based on their ancestry or heritage, origin or nationality, or appearance and general perception as Black. In some instances, even when an individual doesn't self-identify, they may be identified by social perception as Black. The "political" aspect implies a coming-together with other peoples who identify (or are identified) as Black. The only commonality that we share is that we are Black. All other aspects enrich our diversity.

Even among Blacks who are fortunate to be without pangs of racism in their daily lives- if you were uprooted out of your current context, and placed in another Black community, you'd likely find yourself in a plagued box due to your presumed race. Thus, preservation and protection in one environment does not exclude you from the global attitude toward Blackness. In some ways, Blackness by social perception, carries even more gravity than self-identification: if the world sees you as Black, you are treated as Black. The value in coming together is to uplift how Blacks are treated, respected and understood by global society.

That said, I admit that this purview is largely informed by the United States' context of race. Pangs of racism do exist in the daily lives of the Black American community (even if not for all Black individuals within it). Thus, we therefore think about the Black race and being Black on a daily basis. It's a huge component of our lives. Social perception as Black, as well as, our own self-identification is largely at play in our realities. This isn't always the case elsewhere. Although I want to reposition Black identity in this book, and connect global Black peoples, not all Black peoples see themselves as Black. Some identify with their ethnic group, country of origin, language or accent and other identities that are not at the forefront like Black identity is in the U.S. for Black Americans. Some communities stratify by class identity, neighborhood or town or other ways which distinguish groups within them. I can assume that poorer communities in other countries will most often have majority-Black membership, but it is indeed, my assumption. In the U.S., however, we have made Black = African American, declaring that all Blacks have African continental heritage. Ironically, some African continentals don't see themselves as Black!

The Black group that I am proposing therefore, has to transcend race, move beyond an imposed perception or construct to focus in on self-inclusion within a sociopolitical group on the basis of race, appearance, ethnicity or nationality. However, this sociopolitical group doesn't exclude social perception in its definition either. In other words, if a white person wanted to elect to be Black, but didn't have any ancestry or heritage as Black, they'd be a non-Black ally.

*With all these variations, why then is Black used as the collective title?*

Black does not imply geographic location or any other identifier like complexion, ancestry, etc. It assumes those in the Black Diaspora to have largely been transported and exploited from the African continent via the Transatlantic Slave Trade. To take ownership over the title, I offer that Black is:

1. *Of Black African descent:* Your ancestral line includes people identified as Black.
2. Self-identification as Black: You identify yourself to be Black based on your cultural inheritance.
3. *Social perception as Black:* You are perceived by others as Black based on your physical features. At times, because of our complexities in understanding race, some black members are excluded from Black membership. This is particularly true for people with light to fair complexion who are often mistaken as white. In these cases, I lean on the individual's self-identification as Black to include them within the community.

4. *Includes cultural combinations and variations:* Recognizes that Black is multi-dimensional and a multicultural community in and of itself. It includes, Black women, Black homosexuals, Black Jews, Black Cubans, and other identifiers (religion, gender, sex, orientation, etc.) and combinations of Blackness.
5. *Moves beyond racial classification systems to form a socio-political group:* Considering the above, members recognize that self-identification often combined with social perception see Black members as sharing a commonality, regardless of geographic location, and this group is (mis-)treated and (mis-)understood distinctively as a result of membership within this socio-political group.

What unites the Black group, however, is recognition that Black community members are treated differently as associated with our race. Although race is a conceived idea, it has distinguished its members separate from other racial groups. Historically and presently, the Black racial group has been portrayed in negative light: plagued with social ills as crime, poverty, poor health and lower education and largely disenfranchised in every community within which it exists, worldwide. It is the negative association that warrants a need for a socio-political group to come together to offer counter-examples, advocate for equitable treatment and access to opportunity as afforded to any other group.

For instance, poverty is not a social output of the Black race, Black socio-political group or any of its cultural groups. However, because of attitudes toward the Black race, Black members face housing discrimination, job discrimination, limited access to quality healthcare and inequitable school choice options. As a result of these institutions at play, poverty exists to a great extent within the Black community. Without the socio-political Black group, it remains increasingly difficult to combat these social ills, advocate for fair treatment and declaratively state that Black people, too, (be they Haitian, Black Dominican, African American or otherwise) want good jobs, a nice home, a healthy lifestyle and quality education.

## Black Americans

Black Americans often elect to use "Black" exclusively as their own, replacing the imposed title of African American, and showing some distinction from African continentals. I am urging this conversation to handle "Black" synonymously with "Africana" including people of Black African descent anywhere in the world. We can affix geographic subgroup titles as locally appreciated, like Black Brazilians, remembering that the prefixes can also locally change to include, Afro-Brazilians as members within the Black sociopolitical group. In other words, Black Americans, Black Caribbeans, Black Brazilians, Black Indians, etc. can share a common identification within this sociopolitical group, despite maintaining distinct cultures based upon their subgroup identification and geographic location.

In honoring this group that has been forced to exist, I request that promotion of the diversity, complexities, attributes, histories and contributions of this group also be included to counteract this global terrorization of Blackness. Although Blacks bear the brunt of this abuse, the globe has inherited and regenerated gross ideas and associations with Blackness that must be finally rectified. I am proposing that this solution come in the form of secondary school education in the United States, aligning with the shaping ideas of adolescents, and the central institution we use in shaping ideas, through public schools.

## What's Missing from Existing Curricula?

I remember when I was in high school but so many years ago, we had to read the Great Gatsby, the Catcher in the Rye, The Bell Jar, and Jane Eyre in my high school English classes. Although I have always been an avid reader, I remember dying an agonizing, painful literary death when reading through Sylvia Plath, and had absolutely no idea who Charlotte Brontë was (Was she fictional? Was that her pen name?). I had absolutely no connection to any of the characters, or their stories or the ways in which their authors elaborately wrote out their tales. Huge, gaping problem number one: I couldn't see myself reflected in any of these far-off and distant people. Their lives were nothing like mine and the task to read through their work was as required as was dissecting everything Shakespeare. I was a high school student in Corona, Queens, where every third person was of Dominican heritage, most classmates had parents working on their naturalization and what exactly is a "rye" anyway? Did you mean a baseball field? Could this have any connection to Mets Stadium that's near us?!

Of all the books that we read, Animal Farm and 1984 among them, I most remember Freedom Road. I nearly spun through Howard Fast's pages, describing the plight of Black soldiers who had fought on the side of the Union during the Civil War and returned to face rampant discrimination in its aftermath. Until that point, I had never heard about Black soldiers, their participation in any way other than as slaves, non-people, three-fifths a person or likened to chattel. In this case, we learned of brave and heroic characters, based on true stories, that I had never heard before. I wondered why I had to wait until the last quarter of my sophomore or junior year to get to such a good read.

The general practice I walked into as a high school student was "white studies first." This included an Anglo-normative cannon of literature that all students had to learn. This became the widely accepted, hegemonic library of text that we had to sift through, whether we could identify with the authors or characters or not. Only after then, could we add multicultural perspectives to follow the white, male, suburban, American or European tales of yore that all learners had to be familiar with. I simply wonder who made the decision that Chaucer was more important to me, as a Black student, than would be Achebe?

With the curriculum demands placed on teachers, we hardly had time or autonomy to "get to the other stuff" so we never actually inserted culturally relevant text to diverse groups of learners. William Shakespeare, Edgar Allan Poe and Ernest Hemingway had to take precedence. I think the biggest push and arguments for this Eurocentric study was to keep me versed in popular texts students were reading across the country and in the fictive small talk conversations I expected adults to have after reading all books I found boring as a kid at those grown up parties I envisioned in mind. Now that I am well into my adult years, can you please ask me how many conversations I have had referencing any of those books on my school system's required book lists since... let alone at a party?!

Why must my (our) point of departure begin from rich, old white guys?! Wouldn't it make more sense to learn about myself, my immediate surroundings, national scope (including current and historical texts), then regional and globalized readings? What type of structures are we keeping in place when we generationally reiterate that Faust must be learned before Toni Morrison or Maya Angelou who write just as brilliantly? The problem with delaying cultural exposure is that we usually never get to it and even if we do, it's squeezed into the end of an academic school year, already informing students that it is "extra" material, and not essential reading in literature or exposure to history. I wonder why Chimamanda Ngozi Adichie's brilliance in comparative writing between Nigeria and the United States isn't seen as just as powerful as George Orwell writing about England and the U.S.?

*Stigmatization*

A huge problem exists in the United States if its Black members can sooner name five Black individuals murdered by police before they can name the same number of Black heroes. I won't use this space to discuss police brutality, but something must be said for the traumatization of Black American peoples and aware allies who survived the very public listings of names of those who died in police custody in the past five years. What happens to the victim then? We dig, deeply into their backgrounds to find their misbehavior, deficit or dysfunction that landed them in death's arms in the first place. *They appeared to be threatening, they questioned authority, they were on the wrong street, they had traces of vices one, two and three in their systems, they committed suicide*.... the list goes on. These repeated tragedies are doubly offensive when they go unresolved according to law. A "not guilty" verdict in instances like these work to make Black learners feel worthless, attacked and undefended. Stigmatization is damaging because it goes beyond creating a dislike for Blacks, it can lead to Blacks, unfortunately, disliking themselves, overly identifying with the barrage of negative images about their heritage before and around them.

Our curricular perspectives of Black identity often begin with the Transatlantic Slave Trade. How can a Black youth grow if their start is a position of pain, struggle and identity as a controlled possession? With scant presentations of positive factors in Black communities, globally, Black youths are left seeking their sense of identity amidst stereotypes and stigma. The media has had long-term impact in criminalizing Black identity, whereas curricula implies it as inferior. In either vein, how are Black youths to find a strong sense of self?

*Distortion*

So, you actually want to teach students that the Arawak Indians of Haiti (and not America, where this guy actually thought he landed), were purely naive hosts to Christopher Columbus and his cronies until they were all enslaved or slaughtered? They didn't resist, or flee, or even sacrifice their newborns so that their children wouldn't have to endure the hardships imposed upon them by these "discovers?" Distortion in curricula is this: in addition to leaving Black students without any sense of agency, we are actually telling them lies. In hopes to gain recognition of this ethnic identity, a hero who explored new worlds…we sacrifice the recognition of indigenous peoples who were already there. Do we really think that the Arawak Indians simply gave up their land, identity, and culture on a whim? I can, however, understand, that traditional weaponry was useless next to cannons and guns and other instruments used for the decimation of native peoples, but to create them as passive submissives to the hero who discovered America?! Does that sound anything akin to later Maroon, mulatto and insurgent slave communities who would rebel against the French and lead Haiti to become the first independent Black nation in 1804?!

My qualm is in the mass instruction of learners of these fables, rather than actual truths or encouraging the critical thinking skills needed to decipher between these truths and untruths for themselves. Cornel West writes, "Yet, people, especially degraded and oppressed people, are also hungry for identity, meaning, and self-worth (West, 2001, p. 20)." Without this learning, we result in the "experience of coping with a life of horrifying meaninglessness, hopelessness, and (most important) lovelessness (West, 2001, p. 23)."

How else has distortion shown up? Contributions of Black individuals have been replaced by non-Black persons who imitated, replicated, popularized, or outright stole their work. This happened in music with the remaking of Black artists' songs on white only television and radio shows of the 60s; it happens in style and pop culture with African

Bantu knots becoming "twisted mini buns" on a fashion runway just a few years ago. If a Black contributor invented something or patented something, their name or identity is never mentioned, solely focusing on the benefits of their creation. It implies that Black inventors, artists, academics, teachers and other contributors don't exist, and are certainly not to be associated with their highly-commercialized product or style (think: who invented the first traffic light?).

Distortion requires learners to take a magical hunt for the contributions of Black originators in a variety of fields. Since most school textbooks are replicas of each other, the first to describe the widely-believed truth on a subject creates the standard for others to follow. Thus, our country was discovered by the heroic and humble miser that was Christopher Columbus, rather than the enslaver who bullied natives and stole their land.

This also appears in the mass representation of Blacks in all-things-negative as distortions in our learning. Blacks commit more crimes, Blacks are incarcerated more often. Blacks are absent in their families, leaving behind fatherless homes. Blacks are failing at schools across the country. Blacks are in poor health. If these are my sole examples of what I understand Black to mean, why would I a) self-identify with said group if I were indeed Black or b) seek out experiences to engage with Blacks if I were not Black?

Some issues do confront Black groups more heavily than others. Along with those realities, we scarcely discuss the largely racist institutions, policies or practices that created such localized realities (i.e. Black communities are often more heavily policed than other areas are, thus resulting in greater criminalization, and further incarceration; vices more popular in Black areas are penalized far more heavily than those in non-Black areas [consider the cocaine versus crack cocaine realities of the 90s]). Contributors of poor health include the poor food choice options in Black communities, and barriers to healthcare like costs of insurance, and quality of local care facilities. Some distortions, if not exaggerated or seen in isolation of systemic issues creating these hardships, are outright untrue. Where are the conversations and studies done on the Black middle class in the U.S.? The educated, homeowning, debt-clearing, two-parent homes riddled across the country? Where are the conversations of the wealthy? Wildly successful? Emerging families and individuals striving past systematic oppression?

What typically happens to a recognized Black leader is that they are individualized, separated from the Black community they stemmed from. This would be logical, if it were consistent across other racial and socio-political groups or even within the Black group. If a single, anonymous Black person does anything wrong, it is a reflection upon the entire Black community. If they are popular, well-liked, successful or anything seen as positive, then it's a conversation about Oprah, Beyoncé, Reverend and Dr. Martin Luther King and a lengthy list of individuals who stand alone and outside of the Black communities they represent. Former President Obama was scrutinized to assess if he was Black enough and American enough, and once elected: individualized. We can always say that it was of his own choosing and his style merited this separation, again, disbarring the reality that he would have been entirely ostracized in wider society if he elected to reference his sociopolitical group membership any further. This form of distortion, mass produced in media and reinforced in the short list of leaders we share in curricula again and again informs students that Black is distinct or separate from successful or contributing. Since we like naming things, I'd call this type of distortion *tokenism* or *exceptionalism.* This doesn't exclusively happen within curricula, more so in dialogue with other people and is mentioned as an aside below.

> *Tokenizing (Black) people means to observe and interact with them from one dimension. For instance, I know plenty of people who only talk to me about race and ask a litany of questions around Blackness and racism. I am tokenized when my personal experience or perspective is then magnified as the example for Blacks. It sucks to have to account for your entire race this way, but we do it to Blacks all the time: "Why don't you share the Black perspective [because there literally isn't just one]?" or "Do most Blacks… [How could I know the answer to that*

*question any more than you?]?" or other ways that require you to speak for your group as if you know each of the members in it personally. This is a fail each and every time. I can't speak for all Black people, won't try to and hope you will soon realize that I shouldn't be required to.*

Even more annoying is exceptionalism. Oh, so this Black is hyper-talented in arts, athletics, childcare, home cleaning, oration or any other dumb ideas that we, on the basis of our race, are better than. Yes, we are highly skilled…individuals. We are capable of greatness inclusive of our race. But am I a better cook because of my race? Am I a better lover? Am I better at keeping a house clean?! All of these are big ole maybes, dependent on the person. But the idea that Blackness comes with hidden super talents is exoticizing and gross. Further, the praise given to outstanding figures is accompanied with shock that they are Black, then removal as a Black member into some echelon of mononomous Black group that can't sit with the rest of us like Oprah, Stedmond, Gayle, Barack, Rihanna, Jay-Z, Drake or Jidenna. We are assumed to have super abilities because we are Black, but once the general public becomes aware of our talents that Black label must be squashed down or ignored.

*Omission*

The last crime of them all is an outright erasure of the Black identity, in other words informing students from all backgrounds that Blacks have not contributed to society in any way.

- Three Black female mathematicians send the first astronauts into space and we have no idea until a 2017 film hits theaters.
- Nigeria boasts some of the most brilliant authors and musical artists…who never make mainstream and aren't given space in the curriculum.
- The presence of Black African contributions in academia is only now being discussed to be widely implemented across college curricula! In Africa![7]

[7] Fortunate to have had brief experience as an academic in South Africa, the looming conversations about "decolonizing" the university curriculum is only recently coming to the fore, more than two decades post-Apartheid. Further, tertiary education is what is beginning to be discussed, thus primary and secondary schools still operate without national direction and commitment towards this. South African universities are stalwart across the African continent in leading university education, yet an Africanized curriculum reflective of most of their learners has yet to be implemented, reflective of our international crime in omitting the recognition of Black contributors both on and off the African continent.

To tell them "it comes later" informs youths that Black identity is not a priority. To harp on the plagues affecting the Black community creates a sense of threat, distrust and disdain towards them. To disillusion learners to believe that Black contributors don't exist robs the Black community of their histories, and to exclude Black identity altogether, save a few common names and acts, leaves much to be desired in developing understanding of Black identity or Black peoples.

# 3 IDENTIFY THE PROBLEM

## Black Identity Development and Malcolm X

Before we dive further into what an African-centered school model can look like, I want to take time to explore its potential influence upon Black youth. To do so, understanding the developmental experience of Black youth becomes extremely important. A Princeton-educated Ph.D., William Cross, provides one of the best theoretical models for the unique identity development process as experienced by Blacks. In his work, he focuses on Black Americans, thus Black identity in this section focuses in the United States. In the early seventies, Cross identified a five-stage theory called the Psychology of Nigresence, also known as the Nigresence Model or the Negro-to-Black Conversion experience. In it, Dr. Cross describes the stages through which an individual progresses and regresses throughout the model to identify as Black and interact within a diverse and multicultural world. These five sequential phases include the *pre-encounter, encounter, immersion-emersion, internalization*, and *internalization commitment* stages:

Stages in the Nigresence Model (Cross, 1971):

1. Pre-Encounter: An individual is generally unaware of their race or (mis-) treatment associated with it; they have not yet experienced racial confrontation.
2. Encounter: An event or experience when an individual can identify differential treatment on the basis of race or complexion.
3. Immersion-Emersion: The individual seeks to connect to Black identity, usually by separating from anything seen as non-Black to assert their Blackness. The learner is desperately eager to gain more information and connection to their Black identity.
4. Internalization: The Black individual has become aware of their own identity enough to create relationships with people who are not Black and within diverse communities. However, they still maintain a strong protectiveness over "Blackness," what Black is and what Black isn't. The definition of Black identity remains a concrete frame used to identify who fits within its parameters.
5. Internalization Commitment: The Black individual embraces their own identity and can see value in the identities of others without feeling insecure or fearful of losing their awareness of self. They comfortably

> conduct activities which seek equality for their racial group.

One of the greatest examples of how one moves through the process of identity development is in the biographical account of the renowned activist Malcolm X. While written to retell the story and upbringing of one of the most controversial world figures, Alex Haley's narrative finely walks the reader through the process of ethnic identity development according to the Nigresence model (Haley, 1987). I will use Malcolm X's story to illustrate each of Dr. Cross' distinct stages in Black identity development (St. Vil, 2009). Similarly, I can find my own course within these stages as well, and attempt to describe them below. I offer that both the Cross theory, as well as, applied examples help to gather deeper understanding of what Black youths may experience in middle and high school grades, significant for any educator working with them.

*Pre-Encounter*

Cross' pre-encounter stage emphasizes how approval is sought from the white mainstream. The developing youth may adopt practices that attempt to have them appear "more white." Malcolm Little (later to become the world-famous Malcolm X) was pleased after using an intense lye relaxer to straighten his natural and curled hair to appear more white. Although he had nearly burned his scalp, he was satisfied that his hair hung limply, and looked more like "the white man's hair." This sounds almost identical to the exotic compulsion even I had to make sure my own hair flowed like my Spanish friends, was never wooly, never untamed. In both cases, we were generally unaware of our race, but knew enough about society's racial tiers to know traditionally Black features (like wooly hair) was not preferable.

*Encounter*

In the encounter stage a traumatic experience or crisis highlights the youth's racial identity, invoking thought about their own racial and/or ethnic background. This initial recognition of racial difference is often instigated by a painful, traumatic or shocking event in regards to one's own race. This can be introduced by recognition of unfair treatment in the classroom as compared to racial counterparts and a belief that such maltreatment is related to race and racial discrimination. For instance, North American scholar W.E.B. Du Bois recalled his initial encounter and recognition of his Blackness after a rejection from a white classmate in his classic, The Souls of Black Folk (DuBois, 1989). This can initiate a period of internal rejection after reactions of anger, sadness and disappointment. Malcolm Little (later becoming Malcolm X), while a stellar student, recollected his disappointment after his favorite teacher discouraged him from pursuing the field of a law because he was a "nigger":

> It was a surprising thing that I had never thought of it that way before, but I realized that whatever I wasn't, I was smarter than nearly all

> of those white kids. But apparently, I was still not intelligent enough, in their eyes, to become whatever I wanted to be. It was then that I began to change- inside. I drew away from white people.... I came to class, and I answered when called upon. It became a physical strain simply to sit in Mr. Ostrowski's class. Where "nigger" had slipped off my back before, wherever I heard it now, I stopped and looked at whoever said it.

My own introduction to race and racial standards of Black identity occurred when I was a freshman at Washington Irving High School. I was confronted daily with expectations of my abilities and behavior on the basis of my race. The ironic part was that these stereotypes were conveyed to me by my fellow Black classmates who had inherited much of the stigmas associated with Blackness displayed in the news and in the media at the time. With little to no outlets of positive Black expression, we were left to our own (mis-) understandings of Black identity as early teenagers.

*Immersion-Emersion*

When youths become fully engaged in their own race and the Black experience, they are in the immersion-emersion phase. This can be marked by a dissociation with anything non-Black, and/or presented as white or European. As Malcolm X continued the process of ethnic identity development, his active engagement within the Black-led Nation of

Islam was sparked by an intense reconnection with his Black identity. As he grappled with his heightened understanding of his own Black identity and the dynamics of racism, he grew further involved in the Black-centered Nation.

At age 19, I took my first course in Black Studies. Before the semester was over, I would read anything and everything about Black American and African lives and cultures I could get my hands on. I stopped perming my hair, began to wear headwraps, and read as many Black classics as I could beyond all the texts assigned in my course syllabi. As a college sophomore, I proudly declared a minor degree in African & African-American Studies, solely because a major program in it wasn't yet offered. I coupled this cultural study with my major in Social Work, intent to support Black youths in discovering positive Black identity development earlier in their school careers than I had received.

*Internalization*

In the fourth phase, internalization, one is both able to appreciate their own racial identity and navigate through mainstream society comfortably, without less residue of anti-white sentiment and romanticism of all-things-Black. I note this time most during my time in graduate school at the University of Michigan where I studied alongside social workers from all walks of life, including three amazing women (who happened to be white) who conducted civil rights work alongside me and the ACLU[8] in Mississippi during the summer of 2006.

*Internalization Commitment*

Finally, the fifth stage of the Cross model is internalization-commitment where Black youth have a deepened connection to their traditional heritage. Malcolm X recovered from his anti-white sentiments after an eye-opening hajj to Mecca, worshipping alongside his Islamic brethren of various racial and ethnic backgrounds. The working world didn't allow me to isolate myself, either. Within a variety of national networks among the YMCA, Teach for America, Peace Corps, KIPP Schools, and among the informal networks of college and advanced degree programs, my social purview had no room for racial separation.

People can seemingly maneuver between stages endlessly, progressing and regressing through each throughout life, and often during periods of exploration as in adolescence. This means that middle and high school teachers often get to witness students' first encounters with their own racial understandings. These experiences may generate emotions of shock, hurt, anger, sensitivity, separation, confusion, curiosity and the like, and must be attended to by the adults privy enough to witness and support Black youths in these experiences.

---

[8] American Civil Liberties Union

## Sitting Together Everywhere

Talk to any major sociologist or other social scientist about adolescence and they'll tell you it is a painful and exhausting period in our lives when we attempt to figure ourselves out. Call it a crisis, a stage, a phase, the apocalypse- it is a really intense time, complete with cognitive, emotional, and physical changes in being, all at once, over a sustained period of years that usual lands around and during the high school years. Middle and high school teachers get to witness these changes firsthand! I once wrote an elaborate section on Erik Erickson's stages of development (St. Vil, 2009), specifically discussing how unique this period of time really is to exit my own doctoral program-by-dissertation. In this case, I will summarize some of the essential tasks that the enduring adolescent (and their extremely patient and supportive community) must survive including expectations to:

- Acquire a group of friends/a squad/your tribe/ maybe a posse or whatever other current social term used to show that they are not utterly alone, and are further, *liked* by people in their age group. #friendsovereverything
- Date. Between race, across gender, over age, through orientation and under a million other bridges and tunnels in romantic discovery.

- Move away from the values and beliefs introduced and/or imposed upon them by their families and parental figures in particular, and develop their own attitudes, ideas, and opinions of what's important to them.
- Figure out who they are, as in, develop a sense of self and esteem, among their peers.

Wonder if this process looks any different for Black youth, per se? Yes, it does. Because society treats them differently…from early on. In preschools and elementary schools, kids haven't yet developed the politically correct dance steps to tiptoe around race, but can surely recognize difference. *Your skin is darker than mine. Why is that?* By the time youths are seeking intimate relationships, developing crushes, and other thoughts that make their tweenaged hearts go bump, there has already been a sorting: who is considered likeable? Who isn't? *Why is that?* Over the years and between events taking place between early childhood and adolescence, students inherit social messaging to make meaning of the differences they've noticed. How are girls treated differently than boys? Why are *those* kids always in trouble? A million identities can surface here (i.e. religion, eye color, body shape), but race, and further, darker complexion, remains one of the standards misused to convey what is and isn't valued at school.

Eventually, youths do learn that they are treated differently because of their race (read: Cross' encounter stage in Black identity development). They have this nightmarish incident that calls out differential treatment as associated with their race that shocks them. They aren't invited to a friend's party. They are the least favored dating pick at school. Someone explicitly says a racial epithet or slur. They watch their friends get applauded and celebrated in ways they are not. People make assumptions of them, about their intellect, academic ability, athletic ability, preferred choice in music or home life.

Too many achieving Black youths have been questioned or challenging for showing up in an honors or advanced classroom, much to the surprise of our fellow teachers, who wonder how this student of color arrived there. We tell Black kids who they are supposed to be by the classes we track them in, teams and activities we recruit them for, and expectations we (don't) assign them. In the middle of all of this change and personal development, it may then help for Black youth to see positive reflections of themselves in their friends, mentors and role models.

Dr. Beverly Daniel Tatum, scholar in racial identity development and president of Spelman College introduces us to this concept of the "cafeteria table" in her brilliant book, *Why Are All the Black Kids Sitting Together in the Cafeteria: And other Conversations about Race* (Tatum, 1997). It presents the idea that Black youths flock together in diverse and potentially threatening settings as high school can be likened to be. If we were to cluster the milieu of the high school setting and all of the social tasks it harbors (i.e. making friends, dating, finding your own identity) into a figurative cafeteria for Black youth to wheedle their sense of self out of, it would be a frightening sight. Of course then, Black youths flock to the same cafeteria table as soon as possible in search of protection and identification within their own social peer group... because they want to fit in. Fitting in as a teenager is critical, whether Black or otherwise.

However, what generally occurs when we see a group of three or more Black youths joining together? Is it something that we want to popularize and see more of? Absolutely not, in most cases. *Why is that?* Due to our learned, adult-aged issues with Blackness, a gaggle of Black youths can only mean trouble, so they are treated with suspicion. They sense that they are being treated with caution and fear, that they are being treated differently and are viewed as a gang (and no longer, gaggle) of Black kids. This reinforces that Black students should continue to remain by themselves. In one collective clique, they can shield each other from the shun and misunderstandings of society.

While teenagers are sorting out their personalities, they absorb messages via differential treatment, thus creating a need for a collective space of those treated like them. Hence, the need for the figurative Black table. However, when society's messaging creates the necessity for a Black space then there is also a social pressure to conform and fit into that space. The other challenge in this "sitting together for protection" business is that not all Black youths want to sit at any figurative or literal Black table. They may not want their salient identity (what people notice first about them or most associate them with) to be their race. What if their most salient identity isn't race? What if it's that they are skateboarders and want to come together with their fellow friends on low wheels?

In these early stages of Black identity development, when students have just had their first encounters with racism, fitting into the Black table is not yet complex or multilayered. It simply asks: how Black are you? Are you Black enough? These are the early measures of Blackness. Layers and facets in Blackness are not at the fore yet (think: tell us more about what it means to be a Black skateboarder?). Instead, messaging and differential treatment informs Black students to stick together. These apples are the same, just like you.

*Are your Black students forced to fit into a Black social group?*

*Are your Black students treated differently than any other group of learners?*

*Why is that?*

At said table are additional devices of control and mixed messaging, like the negative stereotypes I once received when I was a suffering teenager. Without much reference in their curriculum barring the enslavement of African peoples and a few select and repeatedly named figures in the Civil Rights era (plus Barack Obama!), and criminalizing images in media, Black students get to define Blackness for themselves. This usually leads to stereotyped images that do not leave room for skateboarders, nerds, or the kids who don't like rap, hip-hop or don't excel in sports. *Black people must do X, Y, Z, swing all the way back to A, then start with numbers* because without any positive reinforcement about Black identities in school or Black-friendly media or societal norms to ground them, these stereotypes rule.

Stereotypes assigned to Black kids, reinforced by Black kids who were misinformed by adult messaging and differential treatment can include:

- We fight. If we're challenged or one of our friends are challenged, we fight. Let our hands and our swift-moving fists do the talking.
- Do not speak proper(ly). That's for white folks.
- Your friends are Black, that may include some Latinos, because they're like our cousins in fighting against the power (translation: Latinos are believed to experience many shared realties of discrimination and oppression as the Black community faces [deeper translation: Latinos can self-identify and be socially perceived as Black]).

- Do not raise your hand in class, agree with the teacher or participate in any way.
- Homework? What homework?
- Master your head roll, keep your attitude on: Be angry, these people (read: authority, white people associated with privilege and/or power) do not get you or understand who you are nor do they want to.

A special note to say that the above are generally the assignments given to Black American kids and culture. By high school, we have left Black students so ill-formed of Blackness globally, they have completely separated from anything remotely African. Without any education of its fifty-four nations or countless languages and various cultural elements, our kids have learned to separate from their distant brethren, misnaming them as "African booty scratchers" and other offensive epithets uniquely given to Black Africans in the U.S. We have our media representations of despotic regimes, widespread poverty, and our figments of misinformed imaginations that solely represent African continentals as clothesless, valueless and developing behind the rest of the world to thank for this separation.

While this forced social group comes with its own pressures, its protective purpose does help to share commonalities and create a safe space for group members within it. Peer group identity is huge during adolescence, even as youths are clamoring to develop their own individual sense of identity.

The white flag surrender in student support here would be to disband the Black table in the cafeteria. Our society has informed Black youths that they do need to come together. To then separate those that do choose to join said group informs them that a group of Black youths cannot be trusted together, and there isn't significance in their talking about commonalities between them. In other words, it echoes that we don't talk about race. Fairly, students will immediately question if other groups are then split up, too. Can Asian students stay together? Are white kids split up? How about the athletes, cool girls, or goths? Are the Black kids the first to be split up? *Why is that?*

If adolescence is the period when we most often develop a sense of self, but your cultural inheritance is stigmatized, distorted or outright erased in your classrooms, textbooks or curricula, where should you go? You are likely to look for others you share a commonality with, who often look like you, like activities that you like or are treated just like you are treated. So, if you come together in a Black peer space, but are then distrusted or mistreated and harshly judged by educators around you, what do you actually learn about your Black identity? How willing might you be when engaging with other, non-Black classmates or teachers?

My implication is: With a supported identity development process, Black learners can move to the fourth and fifth stages of the Nigresence model, where they have a sense of self, identity and are better able to navigate across multicultural groups. We can assume that Black youths being exposed to Black Studies would further alienate them, however, this component in identity development becomes crucial in cross-cultural engagement. The other advantage is that non-Black learners and educators engaged in this work can begin to break apart misinformed understandings of Black groups as inferior or threatening, thus shifting how they interact with their Black peers.

# 4 DESCRIBE THE RESULTS OF THE PROBLEM

Prejudice is one of the inescapable consequences of living in a racist society. Cultural racism- the cultural images and messages that affirm the assumed superiority of Whites and the assumed inferiority of people of color- is like smog in the air. Sometimes it is so thick it is visible, other times it is less apparent, but always, day in and day out, we are breathing it in. None of us would introduce ourselves as "smog-breathers" (and most of us don't want to be described as prejudiced), but if we live in a smoggy place, how can we avoid breathing the air? If we live in an environment in which we are bombarded with stereotypical images in the media, are frequently exposed to the ethnic jokes of friends and family members, and are rarely informed of the accomplishments of oppressed groups, we will develop the negative categorization of those groups that form the basis of prejudice (Tatum, 1997, 6).

What happens when we don't include positive images of Black identity in curricula? What if the contributions of Black communities continue to be excluded, distorted or stigmatized per status quo? Does it really hurt or offend Black people? Does it shape how we, across races, relate to Black histories, cultures or people?

I wrote most of this manuscript in early 2017 when,

- Parts of South Sudan had a famine declared by the United Nations after a three-year civil war in the country. The country was blamed for having created a man-made famine due to poor economic leadership and infrastructure leading to a local war. While that debate continued, approximately 250,000 children were in need of urgent relief from malnourishment and 100,000 nearing starvation. People are still moments and bites away from death-by-hunger in 2017.[9]
- German philanthropists defended the title of their fundraising event commonly called the

[9] Comments shared by Joyce Uma, head of the World Food Programme in South Sudan in "Famine declared in part of South Sudan's Unity state" Al Jazeera.
Retrieved from: http://www.aljazeera.com/news/2017/02/famine-declared-part-south-sudan-unity-state-170220081516802.html

"Negerball" stating that it has been raising funds for children of Africa for nearly four decades. When it received loads of backlash for its racist name, earlier variations of the new name became "Negaball." Glad that was settled and a sense of agency for African children was soon restored (note all of my sarcasm in this last line).

- The United States' newly elected president fumbled through remarks during "African American History Month," referencing Frederick Douglass as a hardworking fellow doing some good work, although he had been dead over a hundred years at the time of this praising.[10]
- The 45th U.S. President then asked long-term White House Correspondent, April Ryan, a Black reporter, to set up a meeting with "the Black Caucus" for him. "Are they friends of yours?" Most imagined he was referring to the Congressional Black Caucus, who would have a leader of some sort, who could be contacted by one of the many contentiously hired or appointed White House aides or advisors…instead of implying that all Black people know each other, hang out as friends, awaiting invitations to meet with persons of prestige like the president who doesn't use

[10] "Frederick Douglass is an example of somebody who's done an amazing job and is getting recognized more and more, I notice." Thanks, Trump, for your remarks delivered on February 1, 2017. We should note that Frederick Douglass passed in February of 1895; just a mention.

their proper title, channels to contact them or respond to communications sent directly from the CBC.

## The 2016 Presidential Election

I'd like to pretend that it all began on November 8, 2016. That the vile hatred for Blacks was an unspoken revolution that seemingly emerged on this gloomy day, but we all surely know that that simply isn't the truth. I remember being stunned by a friend's post on his Facebook wall, "1619-2019. 400 Years. How do we want to respond?" I was shocked by the expectation that we still had to do something-anything in order to justify our existence, gain equality in any and all respects, and finally break these binding shackles of menace and racial hatred placed upon us since the beginning of the Transatlantic Slave Trade. Have we been fighting this battle for the past four centuries?! Isn't it more astonishing that we still have a ways to go in this perpetual fight to simply be fairly treated? I acknowledge all struggles in communities and intentional groups, but we have to admit and recognize the stubborn persistence of this longstanding plight particularly against Black people in the U.S., do we not?

Written in language widely understood by its young urban professional audience, Luvvie Ajayi dedicates a relatable chapter about racism towards Blacks in her widely popular and bestselling 2016 book, I'm Judging You (Ajayi, 2016):

> It is why we have to have conversations with our kids early about how to move in America as a Black person. When we make a wrong move, like not obeying a command quick enough, or even obeying too quickly, it is a matter of life and death. It's like we're playing survival of the meekest, because as a Black person in America, you might die one day from seeming like a threat to someone, when you're just standing on a corner. Your very presence is frightening for no dam(b) reason. And that fear can justify violence against you. The fact is, it is not safe to be a Black person in America.

It is a privilege that I get to read for pleasure as an educator. You know what I like to read for leisure? I read about the ill-treatment and poor regard for Blacks, the disparity in Black communities and the fear and anxiety plus social pressure the protection of both white privilege and racism towards Blacks has produced…for fun. I have read similar accounts to Luvvie's in Ta-Nehisi Coates' Between the World and Me (Coates, 2015) and D. Watkins' The Beast Side (Watkins, 2015). I read an incredible book, Homegoing, by Ghanaian-born Yaa Gyasi, who traces the generational lives of one African ancestor, whose descendants emerged in Ghana and the United States (Gyasi, 2016). This young author creatively writes of a family line through enslavement in West Africa and through the Civil Rights Movement, era of mass incarceration and crack regimes in the United States with eloquence.

Even when I choose to read fiction, I am confronted with the hardships facing the Black community. I find it astonishing that the plight of Black Americans remains unseen and opposed, as if all evidence does not decry the absolute merit in seeking economic, social and political opportunities afforded to other groups. Why would it seem so foreign that Blacks, too, want to live in safe communities, with intact families, values they can identify with and opportunity to live a healthy and fortunate life?

Nobel Prize winning author, Toni Morrison, explains the fear that showed up in the 2016 presidential election:

> So scary are the consequences of a collapse of white privilege that many Americans have flocked to a political platform that supports and translates violence against the defenseless as strength. These people are not so much angry as terrified, with the kind of terror that makes knees tremble (Morrison, 2016).

This fear and threat to white privilege was so stark that it was worth sacrificing the marginalized groups criticized during the campaigns, and targeted post-election. I wrote this section of the book early 2017. It's been about two months since the U.S.' devastating decision on November 8th and about a week since the inauguration of someone I have always seen as impulsive. The past two months have been exhausting, and no matter the niceties hopefuls have tried to disguise it as, this election surfaced an utter ugliness, a hatred and distrust I didn't know thrived underneath the surface of society. I still wonder if it is better to have this ugly now seen, or maintain it at a boiling point under the lid as it has been.

After this first week's "selective" and highly intentional ban against seven Middle Eastern and African countries with large Muslim populations, I can't solely isolate this as a "Black issue" but that is just what I have been feeling since I was devastated on November 8th and demoralized on January 20th. Maybe these same hopefuls didn't expect such abrupt and harsh decision making by their chosen leader (theirs, and certainly not mine). Maybe they consider these actions as grave and necessary in curtailing the country's liberal-seeming direction. But I will never forget how isolated and dismissed I felt witnessing the election of Donald J. Trump. It was as if the country said to me, that regardless of what he has said about women in misogynistic form, Black people in outright racist form, or whether or not he was qualified to do the job as President of the United States- all of that doesn't matter. You (Black people) don't matter enough to defend or protect. In fact, we'd rather elect him so that we can get things back in line and in order, even if it is at your expense, yet again. A journal reflection below:

*I have never felt so hurt, afraid or dismissed and could link it to no other rationalization than racism. Its overt ugly head reared so high on that election day. I stayed indoors the very next day in between fits of tears and laughter-in-shock, but I remember the suspicion with which I walked about New York City that Thursday following the announcement from the polls. I remember feeling heartbroken that my fellow educators would have to turn to our Black students and explain the unimaginable- that your country abandoned you.*

*I remember feeling utterly directionless- what on earth do I teach my "sons" to do now?! I had spent my career preparing Black and Latino youths to seek higher education, stay out of jail, form their families' values, contribute to community, and so on…and so on. After June 2016 and the death count of hundreds of Black men that year alone, largely at the hands of police officers, I began to question if that even mattered anymore. I remember thinking: "no matter what I teach my kids, they'll be assassinated anyway. Hated anyway." I remember feeling unprotected by the very laws I uphold, given each scenario found some loophole to define each incident as other than a racist attack.*

*I have always felt judged, but never so separated…distanced…dismissed. It has made me more private, distrusting and unwilling to reach across tables in an adult's cafeteria. I worry, deeply, about a divided country where communities exist in pockets, separate from their neighbors. I remain hopeful that Black youths can have a sound sense of identity and be successful in the United States.*

It's a wonder then that I would propose an African-centered school, then isn't? This would likely draw an almost homogenous school population of kids who are indeed, Black. Although, I will explain that this isn't the case, I pause us to question: why is that so alarming a thought? We can have all white schools, de facto and formal Jewish schools, but why is it when a Black school is proposed it is immediately considered threatening and something to be disbanded? *Why is that?*

# 5 OUTLINE A FORMAL APPROACH

## The South African Example

*I wrote the bulk of this work while lecturing at a university in Johannesburg.*

It was a pleasure to be there and to say that I felt both welcome and supported doesn't show my gratitude enough. My role was to work with education majors who intended to teach history and geography subjects once they graduated. Through the experience, I was able to model, teach, and lecture what I have come to understand as positive Black identity framing within the high school classroom. Indeed, the Cross model of Black Identity Development looks at the Black American experience, and to generalize its theory so broadly, and cross-continentally would be extreme. Nonetheless, my travels found me at a crucial period of time in South Africa's multicultural landscape and history.

When I applied for the Fulbright grant award to Johannesburg, my understanding of the cultural landscape in South Africa was that they were undergoing a period of xenophobia. Violence and racial crimes were breaking out across the country as citizens fumbled to preserve their identity, protect their cultures and separate from impositions from others. I wanted to engage in a society with racial issues similar to those we experience in the United States, and by engage, I mean to *witness.* I didn't travel with the intent to fix anything, particularly as a foreigner, but I did see how the plight of Black South Africans and Black Americans could relate.

*I had no clue what was actually happening on the ground.*

I read a bunch of news articles and still couldn't fully grasp what was going on while outside of South Africa. Knowing full and well that I am a first-hand experience learner, off I went. My first surprise upon arrival was to learn that the xenophobic acts were largely espoused by Black South Africans themselves. Their distrust was aimed toward Black migrants from other African countries like Nigeria or the Congo. These Black foreigners were believed to come to South Africa stealing jobs and forming a new Black bourgeoisie. How's that for internalized trauma?! We (speaking to a Black socio-political group) had so internalized racism towards Blackness, we were threatened by each other's success for stealing opportunities….in a majority-Black country.

As a response to xenophobic acts, many local universities heeded the call to invite more native South African and particularly, Black academics into to their ranks. Among other ventures, this project would become "transformation" the then hot topic and buzzword of 2016. Committees were formed, task groups and projects set out to broaden the face of academia in the otherwise very white, male, expatriate dynamic that had previously existed. Although transformation was a laudable effort, I could sense some cynicism among South African academics about what it meant beyond inserting additional Black faces in the workplace.

The true topics of the country at the time of my arrival were *decolonization* and *decoloniality*. This idea that former European colonies had indeed, decolonized, by taking back their land and claiming their own nationhood had surfaced throughout the continent over the past fifty to sixty years when the first African countries gained independence. However, the psychological aftermath of having an external culture, language and understanding imposed upon indigenous peoples of Africa was the trendy topic of 2017, titled "decoloniality." Of South Africa's eleven official languages, why did English prevail? South Africa has been called the "America of Africa" in that it has western fashion styles, the convenience of technology, and variety in food and social life as diverse as the people who live there. Its residents are often multilingual, speaking three or more languages. However, it was easy to see the push toward westernized education, lifestyle and language as preferable. Classical eras of racism towards South African Blacks had eclipsed the value in maintaining dual identity in both local South African cultures and the quickly globalizing country and posh universal language of English.

*My university colleagues and students would describe their educational experience.*

In schools, curricula often solely focused on historic British characters, long since passed and quite irrelevant to the contemporary lives of South African learners. Shakespeare wasn't any more effective in a South African township than he was at a Harlem high school in New York. Anything other than the traditional cannon of European scholars had often been seen as additive or an elective that learners could get to if time allowed. English was the operating tongue and students were shamed or even punished for bringing their Zulu, Xhosa or other African languages into the school environment.

Although writing in Kenya earlier in history, famous African writer, Ngugi wa Thiong'o writes of his upbringing that helps to highlight this point:

> In Kenya, English became more than a language: it was *the* language, and all the others had to bow before it in deference. Thus, one

> of the most humiliating experiences was to be caught speaking Gikuyu in the vicinity of the school. The culprit was given corporal punishment – three to five strokes of the cane on bare buttocks – or was made to carry a metal plate around the neck with the inscriptions such as I AM STUPID or I AM A DONKEY. Sometimes the culprits were fined money they could hardly afford (wa Thiong'o, 1986, p. 11).
>
> The attitude to English was the exact opposite: any achievement in spoken or written English was highly rewarded; prizes, prestige, applause; the ticket to higher realms. English became the measure of intelligence and ability in the arts, the sciences and all the other branches of learning (wa Thiong'o, 1986, p. 12).

By the time I landed in Johannesburg early 2017, decolonizing the university curriculum was the talk of the day, occurring in private silos, workshops, and lectures all around me. I quickly understood why the university curriculum was the focus and starting point: I immediately recognized the strong regard for tertiary education and the university experience once becoming an academic in South Africa. Much like in the U.S., a college education provides greater societal access and opportunity. After formal separation from colonizers (decolonization), the psyche of the new country needed to also become independent (decoloniality) and the idea of sourcing a local, national, regional or even continental point of departure was to be teased apart by academics, scholars and students alike. "Africanizing" the curriculum was also often fluttered around me. As witness to these ongoing conversations, a few central ideas surfaced, extremely helpful in planning for any intervention we aim to create in the U.S.

*Local Focus First*

A sound educational policy is one which enables students to study the culture and environment of their own society first, then in relation to the culture and environment of other societies (wa Thiong'o, 1986, p. 100).

First, is the idea that learning must begin locally. In South Africa, there is a stress to have the contributions of South African authors and scholars, across subjects present throughout the curriculum. Regional focus, as in southern African, is also helpful in providing relevant context. A continental focus is then invited, not in any particular deference to Africa, but because it is the continent upon which South Africa sits. Then, as a global member, the focus should encompass global stances. This advocates for a shift in a starting point for learning. It doesn't begin with the West writing about Africa, but with Africa and Africans themselves and expanding from their local perspectives to then contribute to the world, rather than parroting European or even American values and ideas. In short summary: a local/country-specific →regional →continental →global approach to learning.

How could this influence us in the U.S.? In our American sense, then, what would be the local center? I advocate for exposure to African-American heritage as the starting point. Students would then learn of the contributions and histories of Black peoples in their country, then on their continent then in their region (hemisphere) and finally throughout the world to position their understanding. In other words, beginning with "what is happening here?" and "how has that influenced and been influenced by the rest of the world?" are profound questions to consider.

*Finding Value in New, Unique and Unfamiliar Subjects and Topics*

Second is the notion of *what is the actual knowledge to learn*? If we are beginning locally, what is the criteria for a worthy subject in a discipline? What topics should be taught in each subject? In many African universities and secondary schools, exposure to African literature was a separate entity altogether, a study taken on by the centers of African culture, rather than as part of any literature curriculum. This translates in the subject being *something else* or *additional to learn*, rather than core examples of literature in and of themselves.

There has also been some resistance to "Africanizing" hard sciences. How can we bring an African component to physics or chemistry? This makes us question whether only western theorists and theories are seen as valuable. Is it of lesser value or credibility merely because an African proposed a theory or tried a new scientific direction?

If ascribed to Chinese traditional medicine, it's regarded as holistic practice. People travel everyhwhee in Asia seeking naturalistic healing seen as unique, exotic, ancient and overall, *worthy*. However, African healers, herbsmen, traditionalists are discussed as "witch doctors" who practice hoodoo, throw bones and sticks, fabricate rubs and pomades for illnesses and otherwise, make it up when it comes to traditional medicines. Where do we draw the line between identifying fallacy in a theory or idea and "throwing the bathwater out with the baby," reducing valuable ideas in African medicine to nonsensical fables?

To create a sense of value and worthiness across disciplines and subjects with reference to African communities is to go beyond merely substituting content in existing curriculum. We can't merely start reading African authors, learning Kiswahili and discussing the economics of the Central African Republic and think that we have Africanized the curriculum. During my time in South Africa, I came across a number of readings that helped to influence my thinking about how culture can (or cannot) be valued within curricula. Three recent news quotes strike me here:

"...But decolonizing the curriculum is far more nuanced than replacing theorists and authors."[11]

With regards to South Africa:

"...Black students also complain that their own lived experience isn't reflected in lecture halls. In the old colonial fashion, they are the "other," not recognized and valued unless they conform.[12]

With regards to the United States and the "marginalized status" of some groups:

"The problem that African-American students face is the constant devaluation of their culture both in school and in the larger society (Cummins, 2015, p277)."[13]

---

[11] Mgqwashu, E. (2016, August). Universities can't decolonize the curriculum without defining it first. *The Conversation.* Retrieved from: https://theconversation.com/universities-cant-decolonise-the-curriculum-without-defining-it-first-63948

[12] Heleta, S. (2016, November). Decolonisation: Academics must change what they teach, and how. The Conversation. Retrieved from: https://theconversation.com/academics-must-change-what-they-teach-and-how-68080

[13] Ladson-Billings, G. (1995). Toward a Theory of Culturally-Relevant Pedagogy. *American Educational Research Journal,* 485 found in Cummins, J. (2015). How to reverse a legacy of exclusion? Identifying high-impact eucational responses. *Language and Education* Vol. 29 No.3 pp277.

*Approach to Study*

Yes, we are citizens of the world and its many histories, but after centuries of having consistently omitted or distorted Black identity, some time can be spent sharing new perspectives, angles, authors, and ideas with increased curiosity towards it than offered previously. Beyond this receipt of new information is a sense of relevance: how does this academic contribution impact my life, world and purview from the lens of a learner? Applicability can be helpful in synthesizing global and historical knowledge in ways that include and engage the perspective of the learner, have them be seen and made visible in content, and begin to see their local identity reflected in a larger, and global context.

*I will pause here to also add the significance of positive contribution.*

I don't mean to romanticize Africana or become idealistic in our coming to a new understanding of Black identity. Nonetheless, if regarded at all, it has previously been in negative light. The results have been continued racism towards Blackness, general misunderstanding and devaluation of Black anything, and a damaged Black psyche. A way to respond to generations of this abuse and trauma is to finally focus our attention towards the ways in which Black peoples have helped, healed and contributed to the development of the world. We have had inventors and protestors, public figures and servant leaders, mass movements and dramatic gains in addition to the woes, turmoil and struggle we have constantly harped on until this point exist within Black communities.

## Existing ACE Programs

*I find myself in the middle pretty often.*

Not in the way of ambivalence or indecisiveness, but I share multiple roles that influence my perspective: I am an academic and an educator, a teacher and a social worker, a supreme nerd…who can also go with the flow. In this case, I am in between writing for a scholarly audience and great people who want to do right by their students. I think about the words to use, oscillating between jargon and casual speech. I toggle between conducting formal research via study and searching the web for some general facts to share as I write this. In this instance, Google won!

All that said, it makes perfect sense to have looked into existing African-centered schools and programs in writing this book. Scholars have been writing about race, Black identity, Black agency and education for decades-plus. I could collect, compile, reference and write a new dissertation on the work. Instead, I wanted to conduct a simple search: What (or where) are African-centered programs in the U.S.? Where can I go to find them if I were a parent who wanted to send my child to a culturally-centered school or a teacher interested in culturally-responsive work? Thus, a quick search on the widely accessible, mildly questionable, but far reaching World Wide Web. I did a quick search for "African-centered education" to get a feel of the current landscape of ACE schools in the field. Of course, there's a million hits in nanoseconds, and many an "o" in the Google search index to click through. After a general search, I came across ten African schools and began to create a pattern of themes across them.

Here's what I found:

1. The oldest among these ten ACE schools were founded in the early 70s, with two in the sample opened in 1974.
2. Most (7) had an African-influenced name or word in their title. Sometimes it was in an African language, others included names of major Black figures, like Kwame Nkrumah or Betty Shabazz.
3. Philadelphia had three ACE schools, Chicago had two, the rest had one school each in Milwaukee, Baltimore, Atlanta, Richmond and Washington, D.C.[14]
4. Only three were public schools, all charter options, while the others were private programs.
5. Only two served grades 9-12, most others were K-8.

---

[14] I imagine there may be a few more, but leaned on the quick find of Google. Parents, families and prospective educators seeking new roles should be able to find ACE schools prettily easily, right?

6. Many were afterschool and summer programs, without a full-time school program.
7. One was an entirely virtual ACE program!
8. Most were led by educators with twenty-
9. plus years in education or doctorates in education or related fields.
10. Most program descriptions or mission statements included a moral, ethical or behavioral focus to support the social-emotional needs of learners.
11. School data available often reported more than 90% of students as Black/African American.
12. Many linked joint and intersecting focuses, beyond cultural enrichment, to include other subjects like science, math and technology.
13. There wasn't a central pattern or approach in attire; some schools wore African attire as uniform, others didn't have required dress at all.
14. There was a heavy influence and engagement with West Africa, in particular, among staff profiles, school names, and programs offered. There were also interests in Kemet (Ancient Egypt) the Nguzo Saba drawn from the Seven Principles of Kwanzaa and smatterings of words in Kiswahili.
15. I chatted with a friend who had worked at an African-centered K-12 school, similar to many of the others just described, but not as easy to find online. This school also provided free counseling to their students, again speaking to the socio-emotional needs of their learners as unique when compared to other student populations.

I rest on the work of the leaders who have preceded me in identifying the need for African-centered education and working in their respective cities to create relevant programs. I learned a lot in this simple search, identifying that these schools and programs have worked extremely hard to ameliorate ills facing Black students via culturally-reflective efforts. However, I find it disappointing that almost all have had to become separate and private entities outside of their respective school districts. This lends itself to dependency on tuition to fund school and program efforts and endless fundraising. Accordingly, these schools do just enough to remain afloat, but their impact is largely local, while underfunded. Who hears about any of them if you are outside of the one-off neighborhood that the school or program exists in?

Within a small scope, these schools are often left out of the educational scene. If you are never invited to the discussion table, constantly responding to emergency and high need, I wonder how your project can ever be sustained? Education Week published an article entitled, "African-Centered Charters on Sidelines in Turnaround Effect" discussing the exclusion of ACE schools in efforts to increase achievement in fledgling school districts (2011). In it, contributor, Benjamin Herold, then of the Philadelphia Public School Network writes, "Last year, at age 69, (Amefika) Geuka walked 1,069 miles from West Palm Beach to Washington, DC, to raise awareness about the need for African-centered education for black children, but the impact of his effort was limited." In that same article, "African-centered school operators have struggled to build collective capacity, he adds, partly because of ideological debates and partly because of the demands of running their schools (Herold, 2011)."

Drawing from the experiences of these ACE entities, and adding my own multicultural training, international scope, and experience in education, I offer a new model in African-centered education. I've gathered these recommendations as an Africanist, social worker, youth worker among adolescents, and finally, teacher. I'll first present the conceptual framework, essential in what I have come to understand of ACE, before presenting specific school-based plans to reposition Black identity in the classroom, curricula and further, high school setting.

## Themes Identified

Three basic themes in my proposed model of African-centered education emerge:

- ACE must involve accurate inclusion of Black peoples, their histories and cultures within curricula.
- ACE must respect the diversity of Black peoples, communities and countries as distinct, rather than one, singular way of Black being.

- ACE purposes to share the histories and cultures with the world as part and parcel of global history and culture.

Lastly, positive reflections in Africana aim to replace the longstanding stigmatization of Black peoples without romanticizing or exoticizing their histories or cultures. Instead, it merely aims to accurately share contributions to a global history and culture, stemming from Black African contexts, that are rarely discussed.

I propose a school model that incorporates these elements as a resort to the general omission and distortion of Africana found elsewhere in secondary school curricula. This would be infused in academic and social aspects of a school or classroom, thus not something we study, but something we live and breathe at an ACE school. As a rising school leader, I am frequently questioned about what an African-centered curriculum entails. Shaping this idea more than ten years now, here are the tenets that I find crucial.

**African-centered education:**

1. Includes curriculum that details the experiences of Black peoples throughout the world in significant events.
2. Incorporates the contributions of Black peoples throughout the world and history.

3. Aims to correct distortions of Blackness and events in history.
4. Introduces nuanced elements of Black communities and cultures throughout the world that are rarely discussed, with attention to unique and uplifting aspects.
5. Values the diversity among, within and between Black African communities.
6. Ensures the inclusion of Black perspectives in ways that are accurate, relevant and multi-dimensional.
7. Attempts to unify Black peoples as a globalized, social-political group.
8. Shares contributions and positive elements with the global community.
9. Asserts that historical events impacting Black groups are also part of global histories.
10. Promotes healthy commitment to positive Black identity development within a multicultural world.

## Academics

### *Approach to Studies*

The critical component in ACE is *inclusion.* Black identity has to be focused upon as a subject because it has been excluded and distorted for so long. Generally, Black identity seen as diverse and contributing to a global society, is left out of school curriculum. When included, topics discuss Black peoples in positions of pain, struggle and suffering. As a result, anything associated with the Black identity is regarded as *lesser than, inferior, threatening* or otherwise *inadequate.* We cannot diversify curriculum solely by adding a few extra book titles or trickling in some Black authors. An ACE model engages with accurate details reflecting the diversity within Black communities to replace this stigmatizing standard.

*Across Content*

To combat what has been previously known of Black Studies in core curriculum, we will have to explore new topics, public figures, regions of the world and concepts with lens receptive to Black identity. It is essential that an entire curriculum be devoted to sharing this new knowledge and approach to learning.

Content areas must sequence these new topics as units across the academic year, linking them to standardized expectation. Common Core standards are skills-oriented, thus a variety of course materials can be used to achieve competency. Black identity emphasis can be incorporated across academic units in order to fulfill the objectives in a given subject. I call the process of incorporating Black identity, histories and cultures in curricula the "Africanization" of a subject.

Below, is an example of this Africanization in the humanities:

| **GRADE/SCOPE/SUBJECT** | **UNIT 1** | **UNIT 2** | **UNIT 3** | **UNIT 4** |
|---|---|---|---|---|
| **9th Grade/African American (AFAM)** ELA - Academic Writing | General Concepts in AFAM Studies & Expository Writing | AFAM Literature & Expository Writing | Oration, Debate & Persuasive Writing | Poetry, Performance & Descriptive Writing |
| **10th Grade/African Continental** ELA - Creative Writing | African Literature & Expository Writing | Writing with Proverbs & Narrative Writing | Oral Tradition, Story Telling & Narrative Writing | Poetry, Performance & Descriptive Writing |
| **10th Grade/African Continental** Global History | America in Africa: Liberia | French/Belgian Africa: Democratic Republic of the Congo | North: The Sahel & The Middle East | East/South: Internal Conflict Genocide in Rwanda and Apartheid in South Africa |

Africanizing content can draw from societal practices in Black African communities, like respect for oral storytelling and creating tales to emphasize proverbs. If a comparable practice is available in the

U.S., this topic can then connect easily to familiar and more recognizable practices. For instance, our American value of oration: public speaking and debate can be highlighted in a unit in storytelling like many African societies. These units can still align with school, district and state expectations in and literacy while incorporating a thematic focus (i.e. African or African-American scopes).

*Across Subjects*

It can still be a relatively looming task to set out to focus on Africa, African or Black Studies without a clear picture of what it can look like in your field. The next section looks at the application of Afrocentric pedagogy per discipline as suggestive ways to Africanize curriculum.

Probably the easiest area of content conversion begins in the humanities so we can continue with this focus first. English Language Arts are generally required across a four-year program at most high schools, and assessed on skill-based metrics per the Common Core Standards. These don't necessarily require exposure to Chaucer or Faust as much as they require the ability to write claims to support arguments, analyze text and other tasks. The texts used can conform to a regionalized focus. For instance, ninth grade English with a Black American scope can surely include Black American literature in its focus. Many of our schools already do this, incorporating Zora Neale Hurston, Toni Morrison and Maya Angelou within lists of suggested readings schools can choose from. An African-centered school merely ensures that a greater variety and rarely discussed texts are also introduced and shared in the same way.

The next would be History. An ACE course in history demonstrates that events impacting Black peoples are just as much a part of world history. It is not a separate cannon or pocket of "Black history." It would also include the major contributions Black communities have made in the world's history and events. To accomplish this well, educators should seek the perspectives within Black communities as contributors to this historical fabric, rather than solely looking at Black peoples as objects to be studied, examined and described. It does not position Black peoples in places of suffering, inferiority or ridden with trials as a separate and marginalized group.

The sciences can be the most difficult and resistant to Africanization. *How do you add culture to formula?* Here, I ask us to consider which concepts have taken precedence across the sciences. Popular concepts in mathematics and sciences are rarely credited to Black individuals, communities, or countries. Why have some ideas taken precedence over others? Are they any more accurate or insightful or merely not as popular when compared to theories from American, European or Asian areas? Why not explore other ideas?

In example, I am a proponent of exploring herbalism as a science. People fly to Bali to find their souls, spiritual healings of all sorts and we call it holistic. But the same regard isn't given to the science in healing physical ailments through salves and balms created by village mamas. African medicine is scoffed at as hoo doo, superstition, chanting and bone throwing. Is there really no science behind botany and herbalism, merely because it's practiced in Africa rather than Asia? Why has the knowledge of one cultural area been given greater value than another?

Students should, nonetheless, have competitive knowledge about popular math and science concepts that keep them in line with the learnings of the rest of the world. I get that. Yet, I think relevant examples can still be used to expound on a topic. In math, how can students grasp a new concept? Are we offering contextualized examples? Have these concepts been popularized by a Black mathematician? How does this figurative idea actually apply in a Black community? Although formula-focused, the contributions and relevance of math or science concepts can still be applied to global Black communities.

*Additional Coursework*

Beyond core subjects are supplemental, yet essential courses, like the arts, health and physical education and exposure to language. In each, there is room to thematically introduce Black peoples, cultures and histories. For instance, the art form of stepping has been popularized in Black and Latino communities throughout the United States, stemming from gumboot stepping spawned during slavery and Apartheid, and traditional African movements. This can be just as physically motivating as age-old kickball. Angolans developed capoeira, a Brazilian martial art that combines acrobatics, dance, and rhythm. The inclusion of capoeira is rare, and typically placed second following jiu-jitsu, tae kwon do and other non-Black martial arts. Instead, we stereotypically focus on basketball and football, heavily popularized among Black American athletes, as the sole avenues of athleticism in Black communities.

As for the arts, the opportunities are endless. Chorus, debate and theater all lend themselves to Black playwrights, musicians, scripts and performers. Students can benefit from exposure to classics and current contributions made by Black peoples. For instance, Kenyans have notable playwrights as does the vibrant oral traditions of West Africa. Warsan Shire of Somalia is an under-30 poet who has performed her poetry throughout Europe, Africa and North America and has yet to achieve deserved acclaim.

Language can be taken in a few directions. We can consider popularity: What is the most commonly spoken language (other than English) in a particular region of the world? We can focus on the student community itself: Where are most of our students from, culturally, and which language best connects to their cultural backgrounds? Or we can choose popular African languages that students may have heard of and are likely to be unable to get training in elsewhere. The key is to ensure that, regardless of the language selected, students are able to get beginners' through advanced levels of training. If we can't teach at least three levels of Jamaican Patois, or evaluate proficiency in it, it may not be the best language option at a particular school, and not a discredit to the particular language or its people.

Throughout the African continent, Arabic, French, English and Kiswahili remain the most universalized languages. Portuguese is also spoken, but in fewer countries. If I were placing an African-centered program in Boston, I would consider Portuguese as a language option, recognizing the large Cape Verdean population in the city. If I were in Philadelphia, consideration of the Haitian Creole speaking community invites French as a language choice. Considering relevance in the school's context and geography, and the ability to teach and assess a particular language at advanced levels, language exposure is a critical way to have students build interest in regional areas in the Black African Diaspora.

*Across Grades*

Local First

I'd like to return to this valuable lesson and point about beginning with localized learning first. I am advocating for an intentional curriculum which allows learners to engage with Black identity throughout their high school program. Let's envision that we are proposing this model in a traditional four-year/four-grade high school, housing grades 9-12. I want to encourage that each school year endorse a thematic focus in learning Afrocentric pedagogy across subjects.

When students arrive in the 9th grade, the focus can be on the Black American experience, whether the learners themselves are Black or not. The thematic scope for the year is "African-American" topics, which can be applied across disciplines. This aligns with our local perspectives, seeking to understand Blacks peoples in North America first. The African continental experience should closely follow a localized, Black American experience, as it is difficult to extricate Black America from its founding African inheritance, particularly as subjects in the first year will include discussions on the Transatlantic Slave Trade and exploration. Thus, Year 2 at this figurative high school will focus on African topics.

With the African continent as the center of focus in ACE programs, this creates and reinforces western and eastern hemispheres of study. To emphasize that the subjects are to focus on the Black African Diaspora, with Africa at the geographical center, Years 3 and 4 (the tenth and eleventh grades) will be titled, "Diaspora West" and "Diaspora East" respectively. This will allow students to engage in Black topics in North, South, Central Americas, and the Caribbean in the hemisphere west of Africa (in the

Diaspora West course). Finally, the Black experience in Europe, Asia and special topics that had not yet been covered can be explored in the Diaspora East program.

## Thematic Scope by Grade

| GRADE | SCOPE |
|---|---|
| 9TH GRADE | Local First: African-American |
| 10TH GRADE | Continental: Africa (as center) |
| 11TH GRADE | Diaspora West (of Africa) |
| 12TH GRADE | Diaspora East (of Africa) |

*Activities*

In Rwanda, a monthly service project is completed by all able citizens as a commitment to community improvement. The event is called *"umuganda"* and entails building roads, schools, homes for the poor or elderly, and other projects in which neighbors take part to support each other. Each *umuganda* concludes with a town hall style meeting with topical performances and community updates from local electeds and officials. Can an American school promote an umuganda-like event in order to meet community service hour requirements and learn more about this East African country's practice?

Singer, Alicia Keys, created and ran a play called Stickfly on Broadway. In lieu of another rendition of Hamlet, could a student cast explore the cultural nuances of this current performer's play? Kwanzaa is a nonreligious holiday which aims to socially connect Black Americans to the African continent's cultures. Can this be celebrated at ACE school in some way?

*School Culture*

Uniforms

We (some people, and on some occasions), present how we feel through what we wear. This can be made challenging in schools that require uniform. I understand how restrictive school uniforms can feel, particularly through the adolescent experience, keen on expressing their forming selves. At a high school without a uniform requirement, I had the good fortune of failing through mid-drift shirts and baggy jeans (I grew up in the Aaliyah era, okay?), metallic frosted lipstick with heavy lip liner to border the edges of my stone-cold face. But this isn't a debate about school uniforms. If it were, I'd advocate for them, highlighting all the positive avoidance of social and class issues that come up in urban high schools. Yes, I am in to school uniforms and get them.

The topic rather is, how we "Africanize" uniforms at the school level. Whatever a school decides, I want administrative teams to consider the frames this places our students in. Uniforms have often been tied to messed up messaging in the penal system. Our kids have seen much of orange, tan or khaki and anything that looks like a medical scrub, but misused as the fitting uniform of an inmate. In some African countries, including South Africa where I learned of this, shorts were used to emasculate male prisoners, requiring they wear boys' shorts instead of pants. Many schools require all girls in skirts and only skirts for the sake of gender norming. A shaven head or a "boy cut" can be taken as protection from airborne infections like lice… or otherwise, in abhorrence of wooly Black hair and more exciting Black hair styles. Shave the head in one country. Ban dreadlocks in ours.

Did you want to wear dashikis? Sure! Be thoughtful that they are largely West African, even though they have since become much more popular across the African continent, for both men and women. Want to create African print stoles or graduation caps and gowns? Sure, but please inform your learners that Kente cloth is largely from Ghana, within a particular region and people. It is not a universal Black uniform worn by everyone of Black African heritage. In this vein, intention is as important as information seeking. Sharing with students the purpose behind a chosen uniform is opportune in introducing new knowledge and culture in the Black African Diaspora. Educators must choose wisely, thoughtfully and with educative purpose.

Headgear

Along the lines of uniform, headgear has also been an evolving conversation. Are students allowed to wear head attire at your school? Also, why do we prohibit headgear in schools as is? Is it in fear? The urgency to see someone's face, particularly in recordings and audiovisuals also available at schools? Why are we opposed to hoods, hats, and headwraps? Headwraps are a noticeable distinction throughout Africa, but can obstruct the view of anyone sitting around the wearer. College students need to see a board and participate in discussions just as much as high school students do, why then do we restrict head attire for adolescents? Is it because we want to control teenagers and their regard for headgear, especially if it seen as a Black style? If we then need to make accommodations for religious practices, why not do away with the ban altogether?

*Staffing & Professional Development*

The staff which contribute to an ACE program is of great significance as each has to value the work, role and responsibility in shifting current misunderstandings of Black identity and Black peoples. This doesn't mean that the educator, themselves, needs to be Black. It can be an enlightening experience to witness a dedicated educator, who isn't Black, yet commits to rectifying distortions of Africana in their craft of teaching. Meanwhile it can be additionally empowering, particularly among Black youth, to see Afrocentric educators who are indeed, Black, as reflections of themselves and positive models of Black identity in the profession of education.

Professional development is crucial, regardless of racial identity of an educator, to restore commitment to an Afrocentric mission, discuss content and curriculum issues, improve design and maintain the focus of the school. Educators need to explore dimensions of diversity, teaching from culturally-centered pedagogy, as well as, curriculum design to enable new ideas and topics and approaches to be brought to the fore. Teaching methodologies and assessment should also be examined to ensure that any program is delivering material in a way that is high-achieving as demonstrated through fair evaluation.

# 6 ANTICIPATE RESISTANCE

The purpose of this closing chapter is to anticipate questions that are likely to arise when discussing a proposed African-centered education (or ACE) school model.

*What exactly is an ACE program?*

An ACE program utilizes a curriculum that celebrates the diversity among Black African peoples throughout the world. It focuses on presenting the histories, cultures and contributions of Black peoples in order to improve popular understanding of Black identity.

*Is it only for Black students?*

Sadly, people across the globe, regardless of race, have inherited and regenerated negative attitudes toward Black identity. Black identity is most often presented as threatening or threatened, marginalized, critiqued, and problem-ridden. It is also lumped into one demeaned category, as if Blackness is one, singular reflection. We can all benefit from improved learning of the diversity among global Black peoples, and improve our understanding of its richness. If we don't, we continue to encounter Black identity with negativity, whether we ourselves are Black or not.

*Is it necessary for all students?*

Yes. Each of us have breathed in smog, a pollutant that has presented Black identity as something separate or problematic. We learn to operate in the world in this way, uniquely treating Blackness with ill-regard. This makes healthy social development among Blacks a hurdling feat. The Black race is a social construct. We then created expectations, as assignments to this racial group. Black criminality is an example. Black peoples aren't criminal because they're Black. Black communities have Black criminals because the world has consistently told them that they were criminal, and set up conditions to foster criminality in their communities. Few employment opportunities, plagued home communities, disadvantaged access to quality healthcare, education and other social resources has created criminality among this disenfranchised group.

Why has this happened? Because all students have learned that Blackness is bottom, recreated over generations and across continents. Once in positions of power and authority, this ingrained tiering of a Black people regenerated, and was sustained as truth. Our lacking knowledge of what Black identity actually is results in a continued space for Black peoples carved at the bottom. The world never benefits from its actual identity, diverse histories or rich cultures. The world is not enriched from true Blackness as it continues to handle Black identity as a threat rather than reflection of itself and contribution.

*Who can teach at an ACE school?*

Any educator committed to advancing education, and promoting greater understanding of Black histories, cultures and contributions can teach within an ACE program. There is a great advantage in the educator themselves being Black, particularly as a reflection for Black learners who needed tailored attention to their developing Black psyche. However, there is also something additionally powerful in seeing a non-Black educator recognizing the devalued status of Black identity throughout the world, and working to improve it. It builds connection, universal commitment, and contributes to our efforts to deepen understanding of Black identity.

*Doesn't regular school curriculum cover this?*

The short answer is: it doesn't. School curricula usually inserts Black examples as additives. We, as educators, often do not disentangle the layers in topics affecting Black people from the perspectives of Black people. Instead, we share the issues that impact them, the struggles they have faced, the select list of public figures whose names we have popularized. We present Black identity as if it were to be observed rather than engaged with, discussed rather than invited. We hold onto shreds of information that have been grated finely, thinly, and without the full and complete versions of themselves. "It's too much work" isn't justifiable reason to avoid repair of our current educational approach to Black identity. To add Black identity on to existing curriculum maintains it in a space that's cornered, small, affixed.

You may wonder if all races will need to be discussed as well. As if we will need a specialized school program for Asian study or European study and other racial groups. Maybe. I imagine that most curricula began as Europeanized study in the first place. We then morphed into something more familiar in the U.S., distinctively Americanizing the curriculum with our history as well, but in singularizing it as one, we eliminated diverse perspectives as contributors to it. Black peoples weren't viewed as contributors in American history, merely objects, and are deprived (outside of one calendar month per year) of whatever Black history could be. Black peoples have been left out in ways other communities have not had to suffer, thus a distinct educational program, a new way of engaging the Black identity, is the least of these efforts.

*Is it racist?*

No, but it discusses race. Said discussions do not teach that any race is better or less than the other, but it surely handles what American society has made uncomfortable to discuss as a topic. It is not a resistance program, intended to teach learners ways of protest or rebellion. It seeks a space of identity in the education curriculum, at a time of identity development invaluable as is adolescence. It doesn't teach hate. It encourages difference and the recognition of diversity across culture, history as often impacted by race. It focuses on Black identity as a departure point because it has been neglected across the globe. Our collective, global "we" has yet to understand Black identity, and thus an academic place should be dedicated to it in the spaces of our training.

We have defined all things critical in our school education, K-12, what is indeed valuable as part of our basic education. I am proposing that a return and replacement of our understandings of Black identity is valuable, for people of all backgrounds to uncover. I particularly handle it in the high school setting to align with child development processes, task-oriented curriculum strategies, and at a time when critical thinking to question and challenge what has been previously taught to us is indelible. This school model is about understanding. The Black Diaspora is rarely discussed in positive light…ever… and that has had severe manifestations in how people have come to learn of and misunderstand Black communities worldwide. We need to create academic spaces to discuss its many contributions.

*Isn't this a return to school segregation?*

One of the central tragedies in our formally segregated schools, largely in the American South, was the inequitable quality of the schools themselves. With the looming label as "other," Blacks were not only separated from their non-Black classmates but given inferior resources, shabby schools and classrooms, and large numbers of unqualified teachers. This education inadvertently meant that we were *less than* compared to our racial counterparts that received better education. That in mind, I entirely uphold a push for integrated schooling, to gain access to quality education, across race and class. But what about commitment to cultural heritage? If we continue to learn in climates that omit and distort anything about Black communities globally, where then am I to go to learn of who I am if I am a Black learner? How do I learn more about Black communities even if I am not a Black learner?

In this regard, I propose a new model. All of us, regardless of race have received distorted messages and images about Blackness, so each student can afford to learn more about the positive contributions of this Diaspora. This setting, school, and curricula can be just as competitive and academically rigorous as others; that this notion of an African-centered program being somehow inferior is exactly why the program needs to exist: to replace this notion that (Black) Africanness is inferior.

In all reality, the U.S. doesn't really allow for an "all-Black" anything. Period. If there's a Black neighborhood, it will be moments before progressives and young urban professionals (or "yuppies") move in, gentrifying the existing neighborhood… or generations will go by to maintain the area as the most dangerous, criminalized and heavily policed area in XYZ land. If it's a historically Black college or university its federal funding and designation as such will perpetually be on the chopping block unless it speaks to a wider, non-Black applicant community to remain afloat. If it's an all-Black church, someone may declare a violent race war (not to speak of the absolute travesty in that South Carolina church and bible study flippantly).

The saddened reality is the U.S. has certainly moved in waves of advancing forward in civil rights for Black Americans…and just as quickly reversing these same and other opportunities. The Black community now remains in an extremely fragile state, pitted between issues of police brutality and further fear of political and social rejection as forecasted by our recently appointed and elected.

Just before racism was accepted as a passable sacrifice in order to restore our country to greatness, we were living in a pseudo- "post racial" society. This claim essentially limited the opportunities for the country to discuss Black identity, its roots, histories, contributions and manifestations in true form. We went from "your culture is far inferior, savage, violent, criminal, etc." to some sort of raceless community, particularly whenever anything Black was brought up distinctively…thus never replaced centuries with disabused learnings of Black identity. This has not served Blacks themselves, who still need critical anchors in their own cultural development and understanding, nor did it enlighten anyone else, Black or other.

Accordingly, that silent practice wholly failed when the country was confronted with undeniable racism towards Blacks. The national election only exacerbated what was already seething underneath the silent surface, and a silent fear and hatred for Blacks began to spew across the country. Nothing had changed otherwise. Blacks hadn't gotten darker in skin. Weren't newly linked to a social ill or ailment they hadn't been before. In fact, trends only showed that despite all obstacles, Black women made astronomical gains in higher education and incarceration rates of Black men had decreased dramatically in the decade between 2000 and 2010 (Goode, 2013). Frightening that there would be progress in this community. What then becomes of the social totem and stratification of our communities if Blacks are no longer at the bottom? Enter Morrison's words on the protection of whiteness and fear of losing its privilege.

> "Every year under apartheid, some coloured people would get promoted to 'white'. It was a myth; it was real. People could

> submit applications to the government. Your hair might become straight enough, your skin might become light enough, your accent might become polished enough – and you'd be reclassified as white. All you had to do was denounce your people, denounce your history, and leave your darker-skinned friends and family behind (Noah, 2016, p. 139)."

If we didn't have social tiering of people, we wouldn't see the graduation of racial classes being promoted to whiteness. If whiteness is seen as an elevation, then it implies that other racial groups are beneath it. Is it not true that the Black group currently remains at the bottom of most systems in this way? *Why is that?*

> "Racism is not logical. Consider this: Chinese people were classified as black in South Africa (Noah, 2016, p. 90).

We have used race as a clear divide, valuing whiteness as the greatest measure and blackness as the clearest way to "other." The unfortunate aspect to this is that Black peoples have then been othered throughout the lives, asked to survive despite global animosity toward them, and relatively erased in history in positive light in attempts actualize Black people as the bottom base. It may have helped to categorize people to fit our way of thinking, but it has destroyed the Black psyche, and neglected to present the value and richness in Black communities to the world.

However, the opportunity to share Black identity, recognizing its worth, has been closed until now. ACE programming encourages this sharing, for all students, to recognize and learn about difference rather than stratification. It will dramatically impact how we consider Blackness and remove our fixed base for Blackness at the bottom of social tier system.

*What will become of the world if Black is no longer seen as bottom?*

## Cited Works

Ajayi, L. (2016). *I'm Judging You: The Do-Better Manual.* New York: Henry Holt and Company.

Coates, T.-N. (2015). *Between the World and Me.* New York: Spiegel & Grau.

DuBois, W. (1989). *The Souls of Black Folk.* New York: Penguin Books.

Goode, E. (2013, February 28). *Incarceration Rates for Blacks Have Fallen Sharply, Report Shows.* Retrieved from The New York Times: http://www.nytimes.com/2013/02/28/us/incarceration-rates-for-blacks-dropped-report-shows.html

Gyasi, Y. (2016). *Homegoing: A Novel.* New York: Alfred A. Knopf.

Haley, A. (1987). *The Autobiography of Malcolm X.* New York: Random House.

Herold, B. (2011, February 23). *African-Centered Charters on Sidelines in Turnaround Effect.* Retrieved from Education Week: http://www.edweek.org/ew/articles/2011/02/23/22pnbk_african-centered.h30.html?print=1

Ladson-Billings, G. (1995). Toward a Theory of Culturally-Relevant Pedagogy. *American Educational Research Journal*, 465-491.

Morrison, T. (2016, November 21). Mourning for Whiteness, excerpt within Aftermath: Sixteeen Writers on Trump's America. *The New Yorker.*

Noah, T. (2016). *Born a Crime and Other Stories.* Johannesburg: Panmacmillan South Africa.

St. Vil, C. J. (2009, December). Training up the Child: Youth Participation & Cultural Pride in the Black Majority Church. Washington, DC, USA: Howard University Dissertation.

Tatum, B. D. (1997). *"Why Are All the Black Kids Sitting Together in the Cafeteria?" And Other Conversations about Race.* New York: Basic Books.

wa Thiong'o, N. (1986). *Decolonising the Mind: The Politics of Language in African Literature.* Nairobi: East African Educational Publishers.

West, C. (2001). *Race Matters.* New York: Random House, Inc.

# ABOUT THE AUTHOR

Cassandra J. St. Vil, MSW, MS. Ed, Ph. D.

With professional background in both social work and secondary school education, "Dr. Cass" has worked with multicultural adolescents for the past fifteen years. After surviving her own rebellious teenagedom as a child of Haitian immigrants to the United States, Dr. Cass elected to uncover more about her heritage while a university student in upstate New York. It was only then, that the future Howard University Ph.D. in African Studies would be exposed to positive examples of her cultural heritage. She has since set on a course in multicultural education, teaching methods to have learners value their heritage using culturally-relevant curricula. Dr. Cass has traveled the world in this regard, most recently teaching at a secondary boarding school in Rwanda and lecturing at the University of Witwatersrand School of Education as a U.S. Fulbright Scholar to South Africa. She aims to found an urban charter high school and serve as principal.

Made in the USA
Las Vegas, NV
16 October 2021

32406422R00073